Animal Blocks Bedspread Filet Crochet Pattern

Animal Blocks Bedspread Filet Crochet Pattern

Complete Instructions and Chart

designed by Mrs. A.J. Lavender

edited by Claudia Botterweg

EIGHTTHREEPRESS
Phoenix, Arizona, USA

Original pattern design by Mrs. A.J. Lavender, first published in 1918
Pattern rewritten, expanded, edited and charted by Claudia Botterweg, published in 2016 by Eight Three Press
ISBN-13: 978-1523993642
ISBN-10: 1523993642
Copyright © 2016 by Claudia Botterweg, All Rights Reserved
Written instructions, charts, photographs, designs, patterns, and projects in this volume are intended for the personal use of the reader and may not be reproduced or sold in any format.

Every effort has been made to ensure that all the information in this book is accurate. If you have questions or comments about this pattern, please contact Claudia Botterweg at http://claudiabotterweg.com/contact

Contents

Introduction   1
Plan the Bedspread   2
Size & Yardage   5
Abbreviations used in this pattern   7
Song Bird   8
Kittens   12
Wolf   16
Fox & Chick   20
Donkey   24
Pig   28
Ostrich   32
Rooster   36
Deer   40
Dog   44
Llama   47
Camel   51
Squirrel   55
Horse   59
Goat   63
Rabbit   67
Plain Block   70
Checkered Block   72
Zoo Border   74
Optional Insertion   95
Hints & Tips   96
About the Editor   97
More Patterns from Claudia Botterweg   98

Introduction

Children are always interested in animals and birds, and no little one can fail to be delighted with a "zoo" spread for bed or carriage.

The "zoo" border may be used for tablecover or dresser-scarf in a child's room, and an insertion made to match for the curtains. Finer thread should be used for the curtain border or insertion than for towels or heavier materials.

The squares, when completed, may be put together with squares of hemstitched linen or cotton of the same size, or with plain crocheted squares. Or, if you would like to make a fancier spread or blanket, join the animal squares with the simple shell insertion that is included in the instructions.

It is a good plan to use the long dc in making these squares: work as for a double crochet until you have 3 loops on the needle, take up thread and draw through 1 stitch, then (take up thread and draw through 2 stitches) twice. This lengthens the stitch slightly, and helps make your work more square.

Plan the Bedspread

You can make a bedspread in several ways. Decide what you'll do before you start, and use the worksheets to sketch out your plan.

Step 1: find your gauge, and decide whether you'll use crochet thread or thin yarn like fingering or sport yarn for a more afghan-like spread.

Step 2: decide how you will join the animal squares together. You can use a crocheted square, or a hemstitched linen or cotton square in between the animal squares, or you can use animal squares throughout.

To sew the squares together: Join the squares carefully, matching the spaces evenly. If fine, strong thread is used, and the needle put through a stitch on each edge, the joining will be scarcely noticeable. Do not draw the thread too tight.

See the Optional Insertion chapter for a simple shell insertion to use between the animal squares.

If you don't want to have to join animal squares when you're finished crocheting them, you could do the width of the bedspread in one piece, starting with a foundation chain of 120 x the number of squares + 5. For example, if you want three animals across, multiply 120 x 3, which equals 360, and make an additional 5 chains for the first space in the first row. If you use this method and use the animal square patterns just as they are, you will have a single-block border around each animal with two spaces between each border.

Step 3: decide which animals you will make, and how you will arrange them. Use the worksheet at the end of this chapter and a pencil to plan exactly what you want. For example: Let the first row consist of three plain and two animal squares, arranging the latter as liked, the second row of three animal and two plain squares, third row like first, fourth like second and fifth like first.

Don't let the worksheet constrain you. If you use sport yarn, three blocks across by four squares tall would probably be a great size for a baby blanket.

Step 4: now that you know how many animals you'll make, and whether you'll make a matching border for curtains or towels, you can figure out how much thread or yarn you'll need for the whole project.

You can make your own patterns of different animals, flowers, birds, and so on, by using graph paper, tracing the desired outline, and filling in the squares with blocks and spaces.

Animal Blocks Bedspread

Size & Yardage

The approximate size of the finished piece will change when made with different sizes of thread and hooks. Approximate yardage needed for each thread size varies also.

The following estimates are for one animal square. Multiply the yardage by how many animal squares you plan to make, and add extra yardage for the border or the thin insertion. For best results, make a gauge swatch before you begin.

Size 5 thread (about 3.6 squares/inch)
  Width: 12 ¾"
  Amount of thread required: 290 yards
  Suggested hook: Size 3 steel

Size 10 thread (about 4.3 squares/inch)
  Width: 10"
  Amount of thread required: 185 yards
  Suggested hook: Size 7 steel

Size 20 thread (about 4.5 squares/inch)
  Width: 9 ½"
  Amount of thread required: 172 yards
  Suggested hook: Size 10 steel

Size 30 thread (about 4.7 squares/inch)
  Width: 9 ⅛"
  Amount of thread required: 161 yards
  Suggested hook: Size 11 steel

Size 50 thread (about 6 squares/inch)
 Width: 7 ⅛"
 Amount of thread required: 92 yards
 Suggested hook: Size 12 steel

Size 80 thread (about 7 squares/inch)
 Width: 6 ⅔"
 Amount of thread required: 73 yards
 Suggested hook: Size 14 steel

Abbreviations used in this pattern

( ) work instructions within parentheses as many times as directed

ch: chain stitch

dc: double crochet. See the Introduction for the long double crochet, which will help make your squares more "square".

sk: skip the indicated amount of stitches

sl st: slip stitch

space: ch 2, sk 2, dc in next stitch. For first space in a row, ch 5, sk 2, dc in next stitch.

block: dc in next 3 stitches.

Song Bird

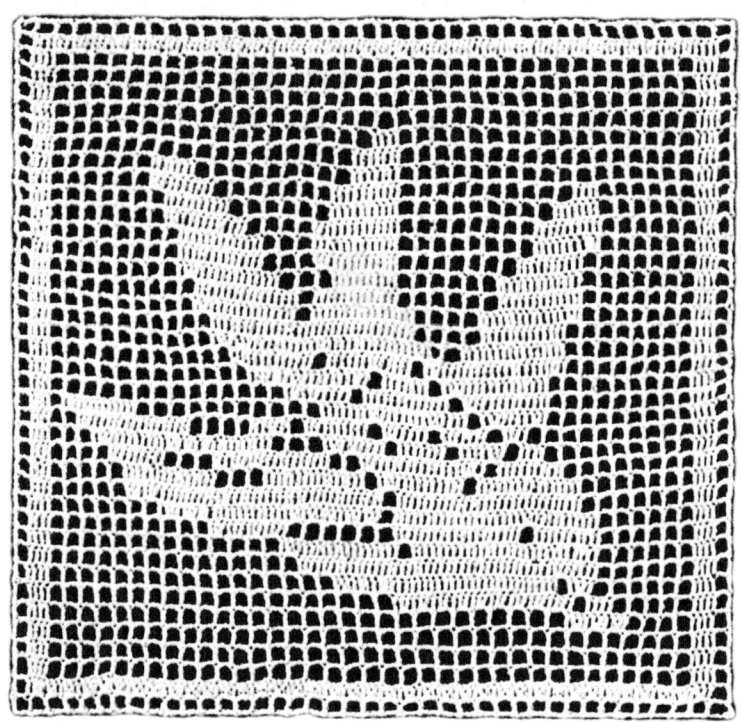

Written Instructions

Chain 125.
    Row 1: Dc in 8th ch from hook, 39 spaces, turn. 40 squares.
    Row 2: 1 space, 38 blocks, 1 space, turn.
    Rows 3 – 5: 1 space, 1 block, 36 spaces, 1 block, 1 space, turn.
    Row 6: 1 space, 1 block, 4 spaces, 3 blocks, 29 spaces, 1 block, 1 space, turn.

Row 7: 1 space, 1 block, 20 spaces, 9 blocsk, 1 space, 1 block, 5 spaces, 1 block, 1 space, turn.

Row 8: 1 space, 1 block, 6 spaces, 1 block, 1 space, 11 blocks, 17 spaces, 1 block, 1 space, turn.

Row 9: 1 space, 1 block, 15 spaces, 15 blocks, 6 spaces, 1 block, 1 space, turn.

Row 10: 1 space, 1 block, 6 spaces, 9 blocks, 1 space, 6 blocks, 14 spaces, 1 block, 1 space, turn.

Row 11: 1 space, 1 block, 10 spaces, 4 blocks, 6 spaces, 6 blocks, 1 space, 3 blocks, 6 spaces, 1 block, 1 space, turn.

Row 12: 1 space, 1 block, 6 spaces, 10 blocks, 1 space, 12 blocks, 7 spaces, 1 block, 1 space, turn.

Row 13: 1 space, 1 block, 5 spaces, 14 blocks, 1 space, 9 blocks, 7 spaces, 1 block, 1 space, turn.

Row 14: 1 space, 1 block, 7 spaces, 5 blocks, 1 space, 4 blocks, 1 space, 5 blocks, 3 spaces, 5 blocks, 5 spaces, 1 block, 1 space, turn.

Row 15: 1 space, 1 block, 4 spaces, 3 blocks, 3 spaces, 6 blocks, 2 spaces, 6 blocks, 1 space, 3 blocks, 8 spaces, 1 block, 1 space, turn.

Row 16: 1 space, 1 block, 9 spaces, 1 block, (1 space, 2 blocks) twice, 1 space, 3 blocks, 3 spaces, 10 blocks, 3 spaces, 1 block, 1 space, turn.

Row 17: 1 space, 1 block, 2 spaces, 6 blocks, 4 spaces, 2 blocks, 1 space, 3 blocks, (1 space, 2 blocks) twice, 1 space, 1 block, 10 spaces, 1 block, 1 space, turn.

Row 18: 1 space, 1 block, 9 spaces, 3 blocks, 1 space, 7 blocks, 11 spaces, 4 blocks, 1 space, 1 block, 1 space, turn.

Row 19: 1 space, 1 block, 14 spaces, 3 blocks, (1 space, 4 blocks) twice, 9 spaces, 1 block, 1 space, turn.

Row 20: 1 space, 1 block, 9 spaces, 5 blocks, 1 space, 2 blocks, 1 space, 6 blocks, 12 spaces, 1 block, 1 space, turn.

Row 21: 1 space, 1 block, 11 spaces, (4 blocks, 1 space) twice, 7 blocks, 8 spaces, 1 block, 1 space, turn.

Row 22: 1 space, 1 block, 8 spaces, 5 blocks, 2 spaces, 11 blocks, 10 spaces, 1 block, 1 space, turn.
Row 23: 1 space, 1 block, 10 spaces, 10 blocks, 4 spaces, 4 blocks, 8 spaces, 1 block, 1 space, turn.
Row 24: 1 space, 1 block, 7 spaces, 5 blocks, 4 spaces, 5 blocks, 1 space, 5 blocks, 9 spaces, 1 block, 1 space, turn.
Row 25: 1 space, 1 block, 9 spaces, 5 blocks, 1 space, 4 blocks, 6 spaces, 4 blocks, 7 spaces, 1 block, 1 space, turn.
Row 26: 1 space, 1 block, 7 spaces, 4 blocks, 6 spaces, 3 blocks, 3 spaces, 5 blocks, 8 spaces, 1 block, 1 space, turn.
Row 27: 1 space, 1 block, 8 spaces, 4 blocks, 3 spaces, 4 blocks, 7 spaces, 3 blocks, 7 spaces 1 block, 1 space, turn.
Row 28: 1 space, 1 block, 6 spaces, 3 blocks, 8 spaces, 4 blocks, 3 spaces, 4 blocks, 8 spaces, 1 block, 1 space, turn.
Row 29: 1 space, 1 block, 7 spaces, 4 blocks, 4 spaces, 4 blocks, 8 spaces, 3 blocks, 6 spaces, 1 block, 1 space, turn.
Row 30: 1 space, 1 block, 6 spaces, 2 blocks, 9 spaces, 3 blocks, 6 spaces, 3 blocks, 7 spaces, 1 block, 1 space, turn.
Row 31: 1 space, 1 block, 6 spaces, 3 blocks, 7 spaces, 3 blocks, 10 spaces, 1 block, 6 spaces, 1 block, 1 space, turn.
Row 32: 1 space, 1 block, 17 spaces, 2 blocks, 9 spaces, 2 blocks, 6 spaces, 1 block, 1 space, turn.
Row 33: 1 space, 1 block, 17 spaces, 2 blocks, 17 spaces, 1 block, 1 space, turn.
Row 34: 1 space, 1 block, 17 spaces, 1 block, 18 spaces, 1 block, 1 space, turn.
Rows 35 – 38: 1 space, 1 block, 36 spaces, 1 block, 1 space, turn.
Row 39: 1 space, 38 blocks, 1 space, turn.
Row 40: 40 spaces.

Chart

Chain 125.
  Odd rows are worked left to right. Even rows are worked right to left.
  Begin rows with ch 5 for the first space.

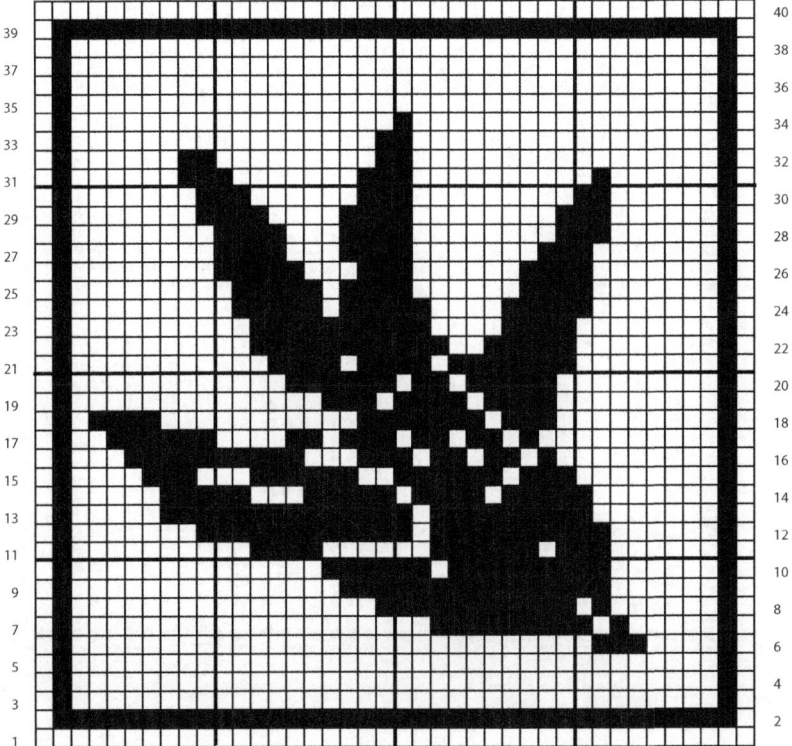

Kittens

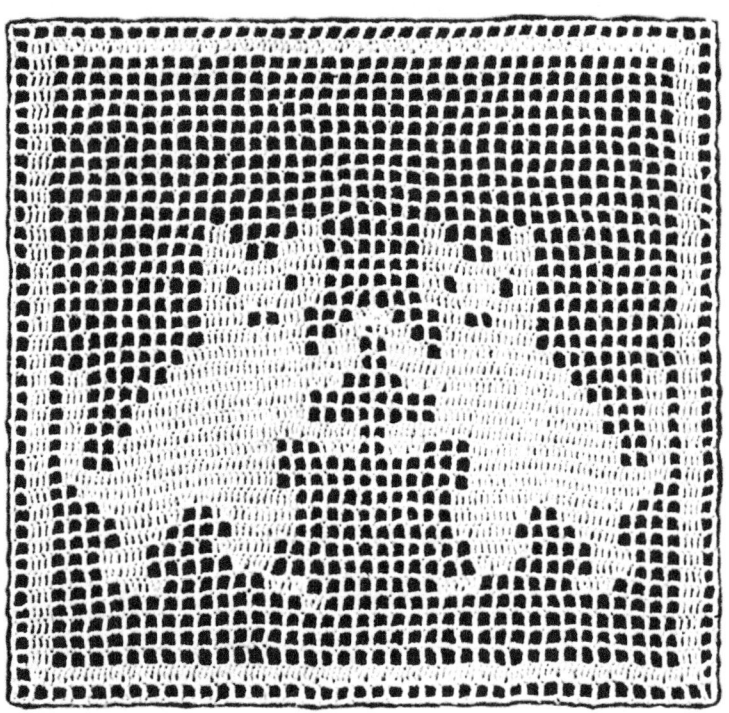

Written Instructions

Chain 125.
Row 1: Dc in 8th ch from hook, 39 spaces, turn. 40 squares.
Row 2: 1 space, 38 blocks, 1 space, turn.
Rows 3 – 5: 1 space, 1 block, 36 spaces, 1 block, 1 space, turn.
Row 6: 1 space, 1 block, 14 spaces, 1 block, 6 spaces, 1 block, 14 spaces, 1 block, 1 space, turn.

Row 7: 1 space, 1 block, 4 spaces, 2 blocks, 6 spaces, 2 blocks, 8 spaces, 2 blocks, 6 spaces, 2 blocks, 4 spaces, 1 block, 1 space, turn.

Row 8: 1 space, 1 block, 3 spaces, 2 blocks, 5 spaces, 2 blocks, 12 spaces, 2 blocks, 5 spaces, 2 blocks, 3 spaces, 1 block, 1 space, turn.

Row 9: 1 space, 1 block, 3 spaces, 2 blocks, 4 spaces, 3 blocks, 12 spaces, 3 blocks, 4 spaces, 2 blocks, 3 spaces, 1 block, 1 space, turn.

Row 10: 1 space, 1 block, 4 spaces, 2 blocks, 4 spaces, 3 blocks, 10 spaces, 3 blocks, 4 spaces, 2 blocks, 4 spaces, 1 block, 1 space, turn.

Row 11: 1 space, 1 block, 4 spaces, 3 blocks, 2 spaces, 4 blocks, 10 spaces, 4 blocks, 2 spaces, 3 blocks, 4 spaces, 1 block, 1 space, turn.

Row 12: 1 space, 1 block, 3 spaces, 10 blocks, 10 spaces, 10 blocks, 3 spaces, 1 block, 1 space, turn.

Row 13: 1 space, 1 block, 2 spaces, 10 blocks, 12 spaces, 10 blocks, 2 spaces, 1 block, 1 space, turn.

Row 14: 1 space, 1 block, 1 space, 11 blocks, 12 spaces, 11 blocks, 1 space, 1 block, 1 space, turn.

Row 15: (1 space, 1 block) twice, 2 spaces, 8 blocks, 3 spaces, 2 blocks, 2 spaces, 2 blocks, 3 spaces, 8 blocks, 2 spaces, (1 block 1 space) twice, turn.

Row 16: (1 space, 1 block) twice, 2 spaces, 13 blocks, 2 spaces, 13 blocks, 2 spaces, (1 block, 1 space) twice, turn.

Row 17: (1 space, 1 block) twice, 3 spaces, 9 blocks, 8 spaces, 9 blocks, 3 spaces, (1 block, 1 space) twice, turn.

Row 18: (1 space, 1 block) twice, 3 spaces, 9 blocks, 8 spaces, 9 blocks, 3 spaces, (1 block, 1 space) twice, turn.

Row 19: (1 space, 1 block) twice, 4 spaces, 10 blocks, 4 spaces, 10 blocks, 4 spaces, (1 block, 1 space) twice, turn.

Row 20: (1 space, 1 block) twice, 5 spaces, 10 blocks, 2 spaces, 10 blocks, 5 spaces, (1 block, 1 space) twice, turn.

Row 21: 1 space, 1 block, 8 spaces, 6 blocks, 1 space, 2 blocks, 2 spaces, 2 blocks, 1 space, 6 blocks, 8 spaces, 1 block, 1 space, turn.

Row 22: 1 space, 1 block, 9 spaces, 5 blocks, (2 spaces, 1 block) twice, 2 spaces, 5 blocks, 9 spaces, 1 block, 1 space, turn.

Row 23: 1 space, 1 block, 9 spaces, 2 blocks, 2 spaces, 1 block, 3 spaces, 2 blocks, 3 spaces, 1 block, 2 spaces, 2 blocks, 9 spaces, 1 block, 1 space, turn.

Row 24: 1 space, 1 block, 9 spaces, 6 blocks, 6 spaces, 6 blocks, 9 spaces, 1 block, 1 space, turn.

Row 25: 1 space, 1 block, 9 spaces, 1 block, 1 space, 2 blocks, 1 space, 1 block, 6 spaces, 1 block, 1 space, 2 blocks, 1 space, 1 block, 9 spaces, 1 block, 1 space, turn.

Row 26: 1 space, 1 block, 9 spaces, 6 blocks, 6 spaces, 6 blocks, 9 spaces, 1 block, 1 space, turn.

Row 27: 1 space, 1 block, 9 spaces, 2 blocks, 2 spaces, 2 blocks, 6 spaces, 2 blocks, 2 spaces, 2 blocks, 9 spaces, 1 block, 1 space, turn.

Row 28: 1 space, 1 block, 9 spaces, 1 block, 4 spaces, 1 block, 6 spaces, 1 block, 4 spaces, 1 block, 9 spaces, 1 block, 1 space, turn.

Rows 29 – 38: 1 space, 1 block, 36 spaces, 1 block, 1 space, turn.

Row 39: 1 space, 38 blocks, 1 space, turn.

Row 40: 40 spaces.

Chart

Chain 125.

Odd rows are worked left to right. Even rows are worked right to left.

Begin rows with ch 5 for the first space.

Wolf

Written Instructions

Chain 125.
    Row 1: Dc in 8th ch from hook, 39 spaces, turn. 40 squares.
    Row 2: 1 space, 38 blocks, 1 space, turn.
    Rows 3 – 5: 1 space, 1 block, 36 spaces, 1 block, 1 space, turn.
    Row 6: 1 space, 1 block, 8 spaces, 2 blocks, (7 spaces, 2 blocks) twice, 2 spaces, 2 blocks, 4 spaces, 1 block, 1 space, turn.

Row 7: 1 space, 1 block, 4 spaces, 2 blocks, 2 spaces, 2 blocks, 8 spaces, (2 blocks, 7 spaces) twice, 1 block, 1 space, turn.

Row 8: 1 space, 1 block, (7 spaces, 2 blocks) 3 times, 2 spaces, 2 blocks, 5 spaces, 1 block, 1 space, turn.

Row 9: 1 space, 1 block, 6 spaces, 2 blocks, 2 spaces, 2 blocks, 7 spaces, 2 blocks, 5 spaces, 2 blocks, 8 spaces, 1 block, 1 space, turn.

Row 10: 1 space, 1 block, 2 spaces, 3 blocks, (4 spaces, 2 blocks) twice, 6 spaces, 2 blocks, 2 spaces, 2 blocks, 7 spaces, 1 block, 1 space, turn.

Row 11: 1 space, 1 block, 7 spaces, 2 blocks, 2 spaces, 2 blocks, 7 spaces, 2 blocks, 2 spaces, 2 blocks, 4 spaces, 5 blocks, 1 space 1 block, 1 space, turn.

Row 12: 1 space, 1 block, 1 space, 6 blocks, 4 spaces, 2 blocks, 1 space, 2 blocks, 7 spaces, 2 blocks, 2 spaces, 2 blocks, 7 spaces, 1 block, 1 space, turn.

Row 13: 1 space, 1 block, 8 spaces, 2 blocks, 1 space, 2 blocks, 7 spaces, 1 block, 1 space, 3 blocks, 3 spaces, 6 blocks, 2 spaces, 1 block, 1 space, turn.

Row 14: 1 space, 1 block, 3 spaces, 5 blocks, 3 spaces, 4 blocks, 6 spaces, 7 blocks, 8 spaces, 1 block, 1 space, turn.

Row 15: 1 space, 1 block, 8 spaces, 9 blocks, 3 spaces, 5 blocks, 2 spaces, 6 blocks, 3 spaces, 1 block, 1 space, turn.

Row 16: 1 space, 1 block, 4 spaces, (6 blocks, 1 space) twice, 11 blocks, 7 spaces, 1 block, 1 space, turn.

Row 17: 1 space, 1 block, 7 spaces, 23 blocks, 6 spaces, 1 block, 1 space, turn.

Row 18: 1 space, 1 block, 8 spaces, 21 blocks, 7 spaces, 1 block, 1 space, turn.

Row 19: 1 space, 1 block, 6 spaces, 20 blocks, 10 spaces, 1 block, 1 space, turn.

Row 20: 1 space, 1 block, 10 spaces, 20 blocks, 6 spaces, 1 block, 1 space, turn.

Row 21: 1 space, 1 block, 5 spaces, 20 blocks, 11 spaces, 1 block, 1 space, turn.

Row 22: 1 space, 1 block, 12 spaces, 19 blocks, 5 spaces, 1 block, 1 space, turn.

Row 23: 1 space, 1 block, 4 spaces, 8 blocks, 5 spaces, 6 blocks, 13 spaces, 1 block, 1 space, turn.

Row 24: 1 space, 1 block, 25 spaces, 2 blocks, 1 space, 5 blocks, 3 spaces, 1 block, 1 space, turn.

Row 25: 1 space, 1 block, 2 spaces, 9 blocks, 25 spaces, 1 block, 1 space, turn.

Row 26: 1 space, 1 block, 25 spaces, 3 blocks, 3 spaces, 3 blocks, 2 spaces, 1 block, 1 space, turn.

Row 27: 1 space, 1 block, 8 spaces, 2 blocks, 1 space, 1 block, 24 spaces, 1 block, 1 space, turn.

Row 28: 1 space, 1 block, 27 spaces, 1 block, 8 spaces, 1 block, 1 space, turn.

Rows 29 – 38: 1 space, 1 block, 36 spaces, 1 block, 1 space, turn.

Row 39: 1 space, 38 blocks, 1 space, turn.

Row 40: 40 spaces.

Chart

Chain 125.

Odd rows are worked left to right. Even rows are worked right to left.

Begin rows with ch 5 for the first space.

Fox & Chick

Written Instructions

Chain 125.
  Row 1: Dc in 8th ch from hook, 39 spaces, turn. 40 squares.
  Row 2: 1 space, 38 blocks, 1 space, turn.
  Rows 3 – 6: 1 space, 1 block, 36 spaces, 1 block, 1 space, turn.

Row 7: 1 space, 1 block, 5 spaces, 3 blocks, 2 spaces, 2 blocks, 4 spaces, 3 blocks, 2 spaces, 2 blocks, 5 spaces, 4 blocks, 4 spaces, 1 block, 1 space, turn.

Row 8: 1 space, 1 block, 5 spaces, 4 blocks, 4 spaces, 2 blocks, 2 spaces, 3 blocks, 3 spaces, 3 blocks, 2 spaces, 3 blocks, 5 spaces, 1 block, 1 space, turn.

Row 9: 1 space, 1 block, 7 spaces, 2 blocks, 2 spaces, 2 blocks, 5 spaces, (2 blocks, 2 spaces) twice, 4 blocks, 6 spaces, 1 block, 1 space, turn.

Row 10: 1 space, 1 block, 9 spaces, (2 blocks, 1 space) twice, 2 blocks, 6 spaces, 2 blocks, 2 spaces, 2 blocks, 7 spaces, 1 block, 1 space, turn.

Row 11: 1 space, 1 block, 8 spaces, 2 blocks, 1 space, 1 block, 6 spaces, 3 blocks, 1 space, 1 block, 2 spaces, 1 block, 10 spaces, 1 block, 1 space, turn.

Row 12: 1 space, 1 block, 10 spaces, 2 blocks, 1 space, 1 block, 2 spaces, 3 blocks, 1 space, 4 blocks, 1 space, 3 blocks, 8 spaces, 1 block, 1 space, turn.

Row 13: 1 space, 1 block, 8 spaces, 3 blocks, 1 space, 4 blocks, 1 space, 5 blocks, 1 space, 2 blocks, 11 spaces, 1 block, 1 space, turn.

Row 14: 1 space, 1 block, 11 spaces, 2 blocks, 1 space, 5 blocks, (1 space, 3 blocks) twice, 1 space, 1 block, 7 spaces, 1 block, 1 space, turn.

Row 15: 1 space, 1 block, 7 spaces, 1 block, 1 space, 6 blocks, 1 space, 5 blocks, 1 space, 2 blocks, 12 spaces, 1 block, 1 space, turn.

Row 16: 1 space, 1 block, 13 spaces, 14 blocks, 1 space, 2 blocks, 6 spaces, 1 block, 1 space, turn.

Row 17: 1 space, 1 block, 6 spaces, 16 blocks, 14 spaces, 1 block, 1 space, turn.

Row 18: 1 space, 1 block, 15 spaces, 15 blocks, 6 spaces, 1 block, 1 space, turn.

Row 19: 1 space, 1 block, 6 spaces, 7 blocks, 2 spaces, 4 blocks, 17 spaces, 1 block, 1 space, turn.

Row 20: 1 space, 1 block, 24 spaces, 6 blocks, 6 spaces, 1 block, 1 space, turn.

Row 21: 1 space, 1 block, 5 spaces, 6 blocks, 11 spaces, (1 block, 1 space) twise, 1 block, 9 spaces, 1 block, 1 space, turn.

Row 22: 1 space, 1 block, 4 spaces, 2 blocks, 4 spaces, 1 block, 2 spaces, 2 blocks, 11 spaces, 5 blocks, 5 spaces, 1 block, 1 space, turn.

Row 23: 1 space, 1 block, 5 spaces, 5 blocks, 13 spaces, 1 block, 1 space, 1 block, 10 spaces, 1 block, 1 space, turn.

Row 24: 1 space, 1 block, 10 spaces, 4 blocks, 12 spaces, 5 blocks, 5 spaces, 1 block, 1 space, turn.

Row 25: 1 space, 1 block, 5 spaces, 9 blocks, 6 spaces, 7 blocks, 9 spaces, 1 block, 1 space, turn.

Row 26: 1 space, 1 block, 4 spaces, 2 blocks, 2 spaces, 8 blocks, 8 spaces, 7 blocks, 5 spaces, 1 block, 1 space, turn.

Row 27: 1 space, 1 block, 6 spaces, 8 blocks, 5 spaces, 4 blocks, 2 spaces, 3 blocks, 8 spaces, 1 block, 1 space, turn.

Row 28: 1 space, 1 block, 9 spaces, 4 blocks, 1 space, 3 blocks, 5 spaces, 3 blocks, 2 spaces, 3 blocks, 6 spaces, 1 block, 1 space, turn.

Row 29: 1 space, 1 block, 4 spaces, 7 blocks, 7 spaces, 8 blocks, 10 spaces, 1 block, 1 space, turn.

Row 30: 1 space, 1 block, 4 spaces, 2 blocks, 8 spaces, 2 blocks, 1 space, 2 blocks, 10 spaces, 1 block, 1 space, 1 block, 4 spaces, 1 block, 1 space, turn.

Row 31: 1 space, 1 block, 4 spaces, 1 block, 1 space, 1 block, 11 spaces, 3 blocks, 15 spaces, 1 block, 1 space, turn.

Row 32: 1 space, 1 block, 29 spaces, 1 block, 1 space, 1 block, 4 spaces, 1 block, 1 space, turn.

Row 33: 1 space, 1 block, 4 spaces, 1 block, 1 space, 1 block, 29 spaces, 1 block, 1 space, turn.

Rows 34 – 38: 1 space, 1 block, 36 spaces, 1 block, 1 space, turn.

Row 39: 1 space, 38 blocks, 1 space, turn.

Row 40: 40 spaces.

Chart

Chain 125.

Odd rows are worked left to right. Even rows are worked right to left.

Begin rows with ch 5 for the first space.

Donkey

Written Instructions

Chain 125.
 Row 1: Dc in 8th ch from hook, 39 spaces, turn. 40 squares.
 Row 2: 1 space, 38 blocks, 1 space, turn.
 Rows 3 – 4: 1 space, 1 block, 36 spaces, 1 block, 1 space, turn.
 Row 5: 1 space, 1 block, 7 spaces, 1 block, 2 spaces, 1 block, 11 spaces, 1 block, 2 spaces, 1 block, 10 spaces, 1 block, 1 space, turn.

Rows 6, 8, 10: 1 space, 1 block, (11 spaces, 1 block, 2 spaces, 1 block) twice, 6 spaces, 1 block, 1 space, turn.

Rows 7, 9, 11: 1 space, 1 block, 6 spaces, (1 block, 2 spaces, 1 block, 11 spaces) twice, 1 block, 1 space, turn.

Row 12: 1 space, 1 block, 11 spaces, 1 block, 2 spaces, 1 block, 11 spaces, 2 blocks, 1 space, 2 blocks, 3 spaces, (1 block, 1 space) twice, turn.

Row 13: 1 space, 1 block, 1 space, 2 blocks, 2 spaces, 2 blocks, 1 space, 2 blocks, 10 spaces, 2 blocks, 1 space, 2 blocks, 11 spaces, 1 block, 1 space, turn.

Row 14: 1 space, 1 block, 11 spaces, 2 blocks, 1 space, 2 blocks, 9 spaces, 2 blocks, 1 space, 3 blocks, 2 spaces, 2 blocks, 1 space, 1 block, 1 space, turn.

Row 15: 1 space, 1 block, 1 space, 2 blocks, 3 spaces, 2 blocks, 2 spaces, 2 blocks, 7 spaces, 3 blocks, 1 space, 2 blocks, 11 spaces, 1 block, 1 space, turn.

Row 16: 1 space, 1 block, 11 spaces, 10 blocks, 2 spaces, 3 blocks, 1 space, 3 blocks, 3 spaces, 2 blocks, 1 space, 1 block, 1 space, turn.

Row 17: 1 space, (1 block, 2 spaces) twice, 5 blocks, 1 space, 15 blocks, 10 spaces, 1 block, 1 space, turn.

Row 18: 1 space, 1 block, 10 spaces, 21 blocks, (2 spaces, 1 block) twice, 1 space, turn.

Row 19: 1 space, (1 block, 2 spaces) twice, 22 blocks, 5 spaces, 2 blocks, 2 spaces, 1 block, 1 space, turn.

Row 20: (1 space, 1 block) 3 times, 5 spaces, 22 blocks, 1 space, 1 block, 3 spaces, 1 block, 1 space, turn.

Row 21: 1 space, 1 block, 4 spaces, 24 blocks, 4 spaces, 3 blocks, 1 space, 1 block, 1 space, turn.

Row 22: 1 space, 1 block, 1 space, 4 blocks, 2 spaces, 24 blocks, 5 spaces, 1 block, 1 space, turn.

Row 23: 1 space, 1 block, 6 spaces, 24 blocks, 1 space, 4 blocks, 1 space, 1 block, 1 space, turn.

Row 24: 1 space, 1 block, 1 space, 28 blocks, 7 spaces, 1 block, 1 space, turn.

Row 25: 1 space, 1 block, 9 spaces, 24 blocks, 1 space, (1 block, 1 space) twice, turn.

Row 26: 1 space, 1 block, 1 space, 13 blocks, 22 spaces, 1 block, 1 space, turn.

Row 27: 1 space, 1 block, 24 spaces, 11 blocks, 1 space, 1 block, 1 space, turn.

Row 28: 1 space, 1 block, 1 space, 8 blocks, 27 spaces, 1 block, 1 space, turn.

Row 29: 1 space, 1 block, 31 spaces, 1 block, 1 space, 1 block, 2 spaces, 1 block, 1 space, turn.

Rows 30, 32: 1 space, 1 block, (1 space, 2 blocks) twice, 30 spaces, 1 block, 1 space, turn.

Row 31: 1 space, 1 block, 30 spaces, (2 blocks, 1 space) twice, 1 block, 1 space, turn.

Row 33: 1 space, 1 block, 30 spaces, 2 blocks, 2 spaces, (1 block, 1 space) twice, turn.

Row 34: 1 space, 1 block, 5 spaces, 1 block, 30 spaces, 1 block, 1 space, turn.

Row 35 – 38: 1 space, 1 block, 36 spaces, 1 block, 1 space, turn.

Row 39: 1 space, 38 blocks, 1 space, turn.

Row 40: 40 spaces.

Chart

Chain 125.

Odd rows are worked left to right. Even rows are worked right to left.

Begin rows with ch 5 for the first space.

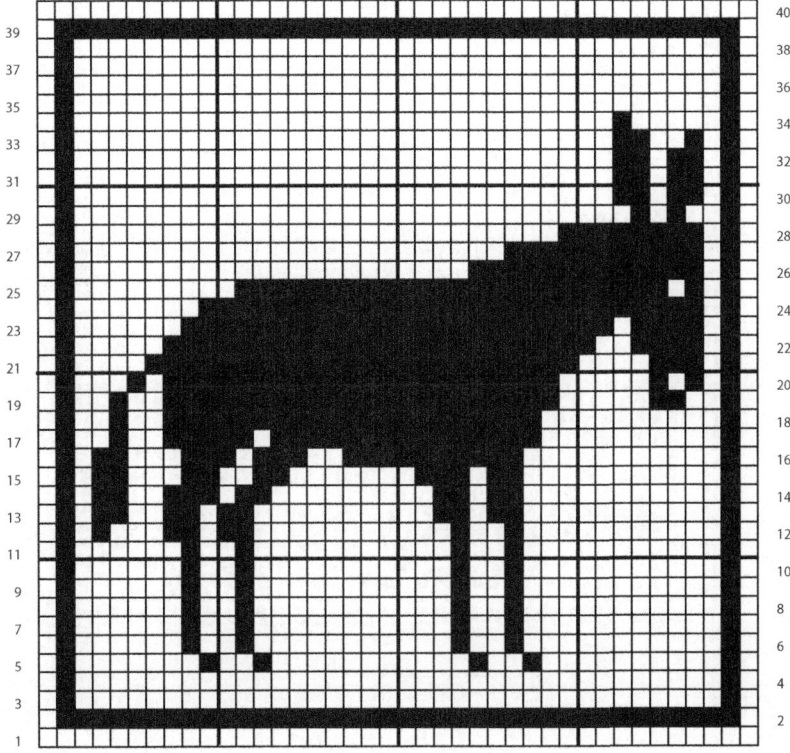

Pig

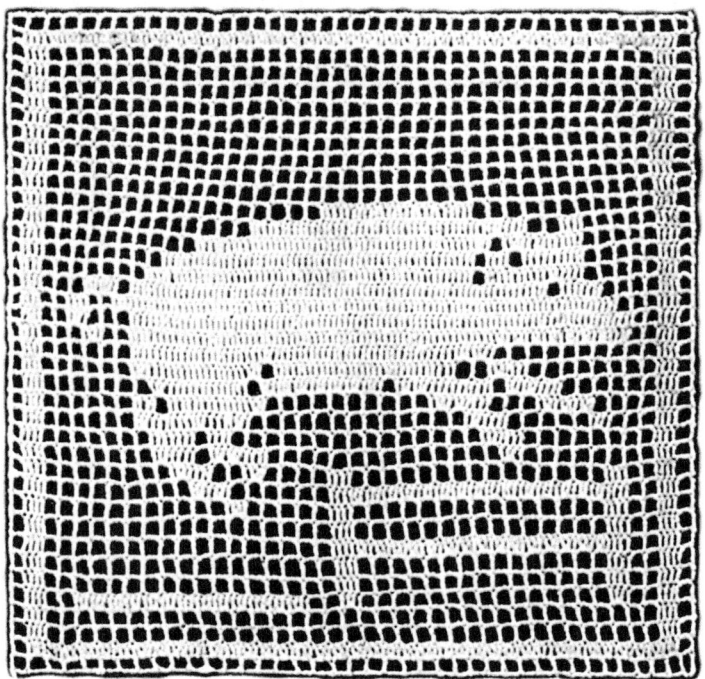

Written Instructions

Chain 125.

Row 1: Dc in 8th ch from hook, 39 spaces, turn. 40 squares.

Row 2: 1 space, 38 blocks, 1 space, turn.

Rows 3 – 4: 1 space, 1 block, 36 spaces, 1 block, 1 space, turn.

Row 5: 1 space, 1 block, 2 spaces, 13 blocks, 2 spaces, 1 block, 15 spaces, 1 block, 2 spaces, 1 block, 1 space, turn.

Row 6: 1 space, 1 block, 2 spaces, 1 block, 15 spaces, 1 block, 17 spaces, 1 block, 1 space, turn.

Row 7: 1 space, 1 block, 17 spaces, 1 block, 15 spaces, 1 block, 2 spaces, 1 block, 1 space, turn.

Row 8: 1 space, 1 block, 2 spaces, 17 blocks, 17 spaces, 1 block, 1 space, turn.

Row 9: 1 space, 1 block, 17 spaces, 1 block, 15 spaces, 1 block, 2 spaces, 1 block, 1 space, turn.

Row 10: 1 space, 1 block, 2 spaces, 1 block, 15 spaces, 1 block, 5 spaces, 1 block, 11 spaces, 1 block, 1 space, turn.

Row 11: 1 space, 1 block, 9 spaces, 2 blocks, 6 spaces, 17 blocks, 2 spaces, 1 block, 1 space, turn.

Row 12: 1 space, 1 block, 2 spaces, 1 block, 15 spaces, 1 block, 4 spaces, 1 block, 2 spaces, 2 blocks, 8 spaces, 1 block, 1 space, turn.

Row 13: 1 space, 1 block, 7 spaces, 2 blocks, 1 space, 3 blocks, 14 spaces, 1 block, 8 spaces, 1 block, 1 space, turn.

Row 14: 1 space, 1 block, 8 spaces, 2 blocks, 15 spaces, 1 block, 1 space, 2 blocks, 7 spaces, 1 block, 1 space, turn.

Row 15: 1 space, 1 block, 6 spaces, 6 blocks, 13 spaces, 2 blocks, 5 spaces, 1 block, 3 spaces, 1 block, 1 space, turn.

Row 16: 1 space, 1 block, 4 spaces, 3 blocks, 3 spaces, 3 blocks, 10 spaces, 5 blocks, 1 space, 1 block, 6 spaces, 1 block, 1 space, turn.

Row 17: 1 space, 1 block, 7 spaces, 5 blocks, 1 space, 7 blocks, 1 space, 5 blocks, 1 space, 3 blocks, 6 spaces, 1 block, 1 space, turn.

Row 18: 1 space, 1 block, 8 spaces, 2 blocks, 2 spaces, 10 blocks, 1 space, 7 blocks, 6 spaces, 1 block, 1 space, turn.

Row 19: 1 space, 1 block, 6 spaces, 20 blocks, 10 spaces, 1 block, 1 space, turn.

Row 20: 1 space, 1 block, 2 spaces, 28 blocks, 2 spaces, 1 block, 3 spaces, 1 block, 1 space, turn.

Row 21: 1 space, 1 block, 2 spaces, 1 block, 3 spaces, 28 blocks, 2 spaces, 1 block, 1 space, turn.

Row 22: 1 space, 1 block, 3 spaces, 28 blocks, (2 spaces, 1 block) twice, 1 space, turn.

Row 23: 1 space, 1 block, 3 spaces, 2 blocks, 1 space, 23 blocks, 1 space, 2 blocks, 4 spaces, 1 block, 1 space, turn.

Row 24: 1 space, 1 block, 5 spaces, 5 blocks, 1 space, 18 blocks, 7 spaces, 1 block, 1 space, turn.

Row 25: 1 space, 1 block, 8 spaces, 17 blocks, 1 space, 1 block, 1 space, 3 blocks, 5 spaces, 1 block, 1 space, turn.

Row 26: 1 space, 1 block, 5 spaces, 4 blocks, 1 space, 16 blocks, 10 spaces, 1 block, 1 space, turn.

Row 27: 1 space, 1 block, 13 spaces, 15 blocks, 2 spaces, 1 block, 5 spaces, 1 block, 1 space, turn.

Row 28: 1 space, 1 block, 11 spaces, 8 blocks, 17 spaces, 1 block, 1 space, turn.

Rows 29 – 38: 1 space, 1 block, 36 spaces, 1 block, 1 space, turn.

Row 39: 1 space, 38 blocks, 1 space, turn.

Row 40: 40 spaces.

Chart

Chain 125.

Odd rows are worked left to right. Even rows are worked right to left.

Begin rows with ch 5 for the first space.

Ostrich

Written Instructions

Chain 125.

Row 1: Dc in 8th ch from hook, 39 spaces, turn. 40 squares.

Row 2: 1 space, 38 blocks, 1 space, turn.

Row 3: 1 space, 1 block, 36 spaces, 1 block, 1 space, turn.

Row 4: 1 space, 1 block, 13 spaces, 2 blocks, 7 spaces, 2 blocks, 12 spaces, 1 block, 1 space, turn.

Rows 5 – 7: 1 space, 1 block, 13 spaces, 1 block, 8 spaces, 1 block, 13 spaces, 1 block, 1 space, turn.

Rows 8, 10: 1 space, 1 block, 13 spaces, 1 block, 7 spaces, 1 block, 14 spaces, 1 block, 1 space, turn.

Rows 9, 11: 1 space, 1 block, 14 spaces, 1 block, 7 spaces, 1 block, 15 spaces, 1 block, 1 space, turn.

Row 12: 1 space, 1 block, 13 spaces, 2 blocks, 5 spaces, 2 blocks, 14 spaces, 1 block, 1 space, turn.

Row 13: 1 space, 1 block, 14 spaces, 2 blocks, 5 spaces, 2 blocks, 13 spaces, 1 block, 1 space, turn.

Row 14: 1 space, 1 block, 5 spaces, 1 block, 2 spaces, 1 block, 4 spaces, 3 blocks, 3 spaces, 3 blocks, 14 spaces, 1 block, 1 space, turn.

Row 15: 1 space, 1 block, 15 spaces, 3 blocks, 1 space, 3 blocks, 3 spaces, 1 block, 2 spaces, 1 block, 1 space, 1 block, 5 spaces, 1 block, 1 space, turn.

Row 16: 1 space, 1 block, 4 spaces, (1 block, 1 space) twice, 2 blocks, 4 spaces, 7 blocks, 15 spaces, 1 block, 1 space, turn.

Row 17: 1 space, 1 block, 13 spaces, 10 blocks, 1 space, 1 block, 2 spaces, 2 blocks, 1 space, 1 block, 5 spaces, 1 block, 1 space, turn.

Row 18: 1 space, 1 block, 4 spaces, 1 block, 1 space, 18 blocks, 12 spaces, 1 block, 1 space, turn.

Row 19: 1 space, 1 block, 10 spaces, 22 blocks, 4 spaces, 1 block, 1 space, turn.

Row 20: 1 space, 1 block, 5 spaces, 22 blocks, 9 spaces, 1 block, 1 space, turn.

Row 21: 1 space, 1 block, 9 spaces, 21 blocks, 6 spaces, 1 block, 1 space, turn.

Row 22: 1 space, 1 block, 7 spaces, 15 blocks, 2 spaces, 4 blocks, 8 spaces, 1 block, 1 space, turn.

Row 23: 1 space, 1 block, 8 spaces, 3 blocks, 4 spaces, 13 blocks, 8 spaces, 1 block, 1 space, turn.

Row 24: 1 space, 1 block, 9 spaces, 11 blocks, 5 spaces, 3 blocks, 8 spaces, 1 block, 1 space, turn.

Row 25: 1 space, 1 block, 8 spaces, 2 blocks, 6 spaces, 10 blocks, 10 spaces, 1 block, 1 space, turn.

Row 26: 1 space, 1 block, 11 spaces, 8 blocks, 7 spaces, 2 blocks, 8 spaces, 1 block, 1 space, turn.

Row 27: 1 space, 1 block, 8 spaces, 2 blocks, 7 spaces, 7 blocks, 12 spaces, 1 block, 1 space, turn.

Row 28: 1 space, 1 block, 13 spaces, 5 blocks, 8 spaces, 2 blocks, 8 spaces, 1 block, 1 space, turn.

Row 29: 1 space, 1 block, 8 spaces, 2 blocks, 26 spaces, 1 block, 1 space, turn.

Row 30: 1 space, 1 block, 26 spaces, 3 blocks, 7 spaces, 1 block, 1 space, turn.

Row 31: 1 space, 1 block, 4 spaces, 7 blocks, 25 spaces, 1 block, 1 space, turn.

Row 32: 1 space, 1 block, 25 spaces, 2 blocks, 1 space, 2 blocks, 6 spaces, 1 block, 1 space, turn.

Row 33: 1 space, 1 block, 7 spaces, 3 blocks, 26 spaces, 1 block, 1 space, turn.

Rows 34 – 38: 1 space, 1 block, 36 spaces, 1 block, 1 space, turn.
Row 39: 1 space, 38 blocks, 1 space, turn.
Row 40: 40 spaces.

Chart

Chain 125.

Odd rows are worked left to right. Even rows are worked right to left.

Begin rows with ch 5 for the first space.

Rooster

Written Instructions

Chain 125.
    Row 1: Dc in 8th ch from hook, 39 spaces, turn. 40 squares.
    Row 2: 1 space, 38 blocks, 1 space, turn.
    Row 3: 1 space, 1 block, 36 spaces, 1 block, 1 space, turn.
    Row 4: 1 space, 1 block, 23 spaces, 1 block, 1 space, 3 blocks, 8 spaces, 1 block, 1 space, turn.

Row 5: 1 space, 1 block, 11 spaces, 1 block, 24 spaces, 1 block, 1 space, turn.
Row 6: 1 space, 1 block, 10 spaces, 5 blocks, 8 spaces, 2 blocks, 11 spaces, 1 block, 1 space, turn.
Row 7: 1 space, 1 block, 10 spaces, 2 blocks, 1 space, 2 blocks, 4 spaces, 4 blocks, 3 spaces, 1 block, 9 spaces, 1 block, 1 space, turn.
Row 8: 1 space, 1 block, 8 spaces, 1 block, 11 spaces, (1 block, 1 space) twice, 1 block, 11 spaces, 1 block, 1 space, turn.
Row 9: 1 space, 1 block, 11 spaces, 1 block, 1 space, 1 block, 22 spaces, 1 block, 1 space, turn.
Row 10: 1 space, 1 block, 22 spaces, 1 block, 1 space, 2 blocks, 10 spaces, 1 block, 1 space, turn.
Row 11: 1 space, 1 block, 9 spaces, 4 blocks, 1 space, 2 blocks, 20 spaces, 1 block, 1 space, turn.
Row 12: 1 space, 1 block, 18 spaces, 9 blocks, 9 spaces, 1 block, 1 space, turn.
Row 13: 1 space, 1 block, 8 spaces, 7 blocks, 1 space, 4 blocks, 9 spaces, 2 blocks, 5 spaces, 1 block, 1 space, turn.
Row 14: 1 space, 1 block, 4 spaces, 2 blocks, 2 spaces, 1 block, 2 spaces, 2 blocks, 1 space, 1 block, 1 space, 4 blocks, 3 spaces, 7 blocks, 6 spaces, 1 block, 1 space, turn.
Row 15: 1 space, 1 block, 5 spaces, 6 blocks, 5 spaces, 3 blocks, 1 space, 2 blocks, 2 spaces, 2 blocks, 1 space, 1 block, 3 spaces, 2 blocks, 3 spaces, 1 block, 1 space, turn.
Row 16: 1 space, 1 block, 3 spaces, 2 blocks, 2 spaces, 2 blocks, 1 space, 2 blocks, 2 spaces, 10 blocks, 3 spaces, 6 blocks, 3 spaces, 1 block, 1 space, turn.
Row 17: 1 space, 1 block, 2 spaces, 7 blocks, 1 space, 11 blocks, 1 space, 3 blocks, (2 spaces, 2 blocks) twice, 3 spaces, 1 block, 1 space, turn.
Row 18: 1 space, 1 block, 3 spaces, 2 blocks, 2 spaces, 2 blocks, 4 spaces, 2 blocks, 1 space, 18 blocks, 2 spaces, 1 block, 1 space, turn.

Row 19: 1 space, 1 block, 2 spaces, 17 blocks, 1 space, 5 blocks, 2 spaces, 2 blocks, 1 space, 3 blocks, 3 spaces, 1 block, 1 space, turn.

Row 20: 1 space, 1 block, 4 spaces, 2 blocks, 2 spaces, 5 blocks, 1 space, 3 blocks, 2 spaces, 15 blocks, 2 spaces, 1 block, 1 space, turn.

Row 21: 1 space, 1 block, 2 spaces, 10 blocks, 3 spaces, 6 blocks, 1 space, 1 block, 1 space, 3 blocks, 2 spaces, 3 blocks, 4 spaces, 1 block, 1 space, turn.

Row 22: 1 space, 1 block, 5 spaces, 3 blocks, 4 spaces, 8 blocks, 5 spaces, 8 blocks, 3 spaces, 1 block, 1 space, turn.

Row 23: 1 space, 1 block, 2 spaces, 9 blocks, 8 spaces, 2 blocks, 2 spaces, 7 blocks, 6 spaces, 1 block, 1 space, turn.

Row 24: 1 space, 1 block, 2 spaces, 3 blocks, 4 spaces, 3 blocks, 3 spaces, 2 blocks, 9 spaces, 8 blocks, 2 spaces, 1 block, 1 space, turn.

Row 25: 1 space, 1 block, 2 spaces, 8 blocks, 10 spaces, 2 blocks, 7 spaces, 5 blocks, 2 spaces, 1 block, 1 space, turn.

Row 26: 1 space, 1 block, 5 spaces, 4 blocks, 3 spaces, 4 blocks, 11 spaces, 5 blocks, 4 spaces, 1 block, 1 space, turn.

Row 27: 1 space, 1 block, 3 spaces, 5 blocks, 14 spaces, 7 blocks, 7 spaces, 1 block, 1 space, turn.

Row 28: 1 space, 1 block, 9 spaces, 3 blocks, 14 spaces, 4 blocks, 1 space, 3 blocks, 2 spaces, 1 block, 1 space, turn.

Row 29: 1 space, 1 block, 3 spaces, 7 blocks, 26 spaces, 1 block, 1 space, turn.

Row 30: 1 space, 1 block, 16 spaces, 1 block, 2 spaces, 1 block, 7 spaces, 6 blocks, 1 block, 1 space, turn.

Row 31: 1 space, 1 block, 5 spaces, 1 block, 1 space, 1 block, 9 spaces, 2 blocks, 17 spaces, 1 block, 1 space, turn.

Row 32: 1 space, 1 block, 17 spaces, 2 blocks, 17 spaces, 1 block, 1 space, turn.

Row 33: 1 space, 1 block, 16 spaces, 1 block, 2 spaces, 1 block, 16 spaces, 1 block, 1 space, turn.

Rows 34 – 38: 1 space, 1 block, 36 spaces, 1 block, 1 space, turn.

Row 39: 1 space, 38 blocks, 1 space, turn.

Row 40: 40 spaces.

Chart

Chain 125.

Odd rows are worked left to right. Even rows are worked right to left.

Begin rows with ch 5 for the first space.

Deer

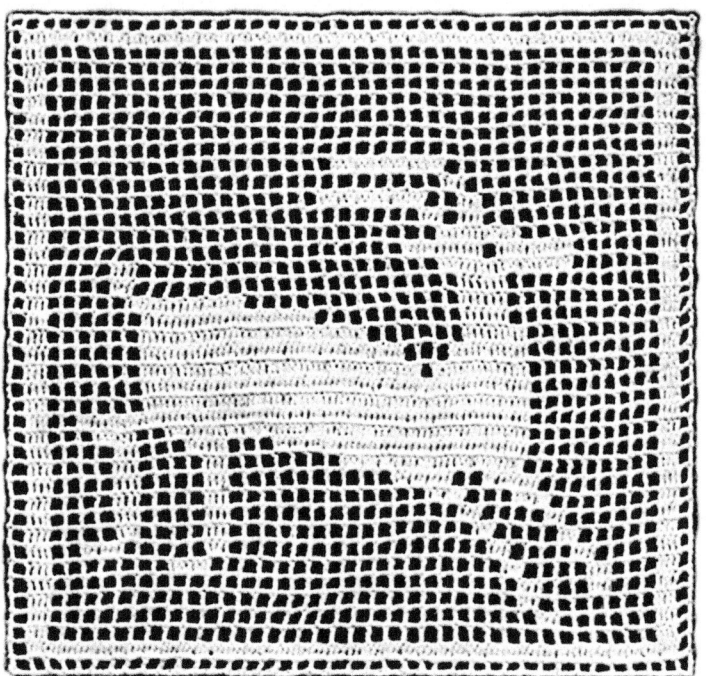

Written Instructions

Chain 125.

Row 1: Dc in 8th ch from hook, 39 spaces, turn. 40 squares.
Row 2: 1 space, 38 blocks, 1 space, turn.
Row 3: 1 space, 1 block, 36 spaces, 1 block, 1 space, turn.
Row 4: 1 space, 1 block, 6 spaces, 1 block, 29 spaces, 1 block, 1 space, turn.

Row 5: 1 space, 1 block, 28 spaces, 1 block, 7 spaces, 1 block, 1 space, turn.

Row 6: 1 space, 1 block, (3 spaces, 1 block) twice, 28 spaces, 1 block, 1 space, turn.

Row 7: 1 space, 1 block, 7 spaces, 2 blocks, 18 spaces, 1 block, 4 spaces, 1 block, 3 spaces, 1 block, 1 space, turn.

Row 8: 1 space, 1 block, (4 spaces, 1 block) twice, 16 spaces, 1 block, 5 spaces, 2 blocks, 2 spaces, 1 block, 1 space, turn.

Row 9: 1 space, 1 block, (4 spaces, 1 block) twice, 15 spaces, 1 block, 4 spaces, 1 block, 5 spaces, 1 block, 1 space, turn.

Row 10: 1 space, 1 block, 6 spaces, 1 block, 4 spaces, 1 block, 14 spaces, (1 block, 4 spaces) twice, 1 block, 1 space, turn.

Row 11: 1 space, 1 block, (4 spaces, 1 block) twice, 12 spaces, 2 blocks, 3 spaces, 2 blocks, 7 spaces, 1 block, 1 space, turn.

Row 12: 1 space, 1 block, 8 spaces, 3 blocks, 2 spaces, 3 blocks, 10 spaces, (1 block, 4 spaces) twice, 1 block, 1 space, turn.

Row 13: 1 space, 1 block, (4 spaces, 1 block) twice, 7 spaces, 10 blocks, 9 spaces, 1 block, 1 space, turn.

Row 14: 1 space, 1 block, 9 spaces, 14 blocks, 3 spaces, 2 blocks, 3 spaces, 1 block, 4 spaces, 1 block, 1 space, turn.

Row 15: 1 space, 1 block, 3 spaces, 2 blocks, 2 spaces, 20 blocks, 9 spaces, 1 block, 1 space, turn.

Row 16: 1 space, 1 block, 9 spaces, 25 blocks, 2 spaces, 1 block, 1 space, turn.

Row 17: 1 space, 1 block, 6 spaces, 21 blocks, 9 spaces, 1 block, 1 space, turn.

Row 18: 1 space, 1 block, 9 spaces, 21 blocks, 6 spaces, 1 block, 1 space, turn.

Row 19: 1 space, 1 block, 6 spaces, 15 blocks, 1 space, 5 blocks, 9 spaces, 1 block, 1 space, turn.

Row 20: 1 space, 1 block, 9 spaces, 4 blocks, 3 spaces, 14 blocks, 6 spaces, 1 block, 1 space, turn.

Row 21: 1 space, 1 block, 6 spaces, 12 blocks, 6 spaces, 3 blocks, 9 spaces, 1 block, 1 space, turn.

Row 22: 1 space, 1 block, 10 spaces, 2 blocks, 9 spaces, 9 blocks, 6 spaces, 1 block, 1 space, turn.

Row 23: 1 space, 1 block, 5 spaces, 6 blocks, 13 spaces, 2 blocks, 10 spaces, 1 block, 1 space, turn.

Row 24: 1 space, 1 block, 10 spaces, 2 blocks, 19 spaces, 1 block, 4 spaces, 1 block, 1 space, turn.

Row 25: 1 space, 1 block, 4 spaces, 1 block, 18 spaces, 7 blocks, 6 spaces, 1 block, 1 space, turn.

Row 26: 1 space, 1 block, 6 spaces, 4 blocks, 1 space, 4 blocks, 21 spaces, 1 block, 1 space, turn.

Row 27: 1 space, 1 block, 23 spaces, 4 blocks, 9 spaces, 1 block, 1 space, turn.

Row 28: 1 space, 1 block, 11 spaces, 1 block, 1 space, 1 block, 22 spaces, 1 block, 1 space, turn.

Row 29: 1 space, 1 block, 16 spaces, 6 blocks, 2 spaces, 1 block, 11 spaces, 1 block, 1 space, turn.

Row 30: 1 space, 1 block, 12 spaces, 1 block, 23 spaces, 1 block, 1 space, turn.

Row 31: 1 space, 1 block, 17 spaces, 6 blocks, 13 spaces, 1 block, 1 space, turn.

Rows 32 – 38: 1 space, 1 block, 36 spaces, 1 block, 1 space, turn.

Row 39: 1 space, 38 blocks, 1 space, turn.

Row 40: 40 spaces.

Chart

Chain 125.

Odd rows are worked left to right. Even rows are worked right to left.

Begin rows with ch 5 for the first space.

Dog

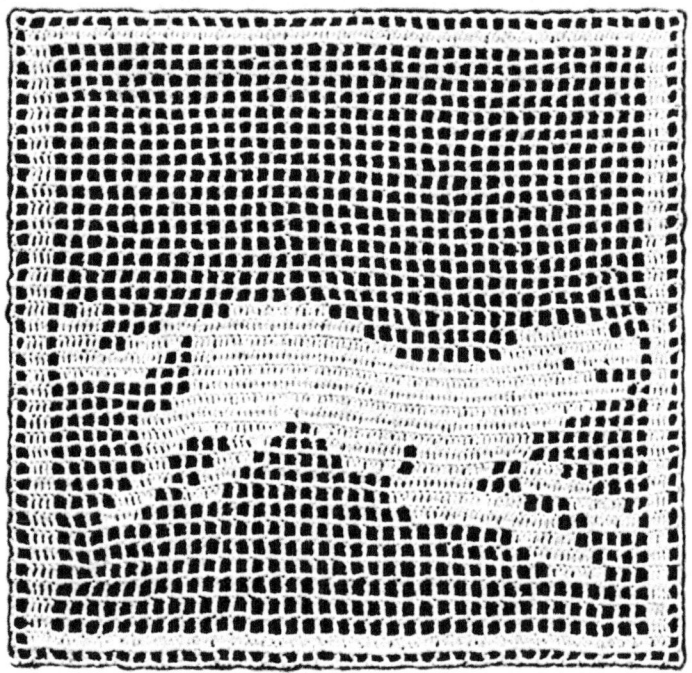

Written Instructions

Chain 125.
    Row 1: Dc in 8th ch from hook, 39 spaces, turn. 40 squares.
    Row 2: 1 space, 38 blocks, 1 space, turn.
    Rows 3 – 5: 1 space, 1 block, 36 spaces, 1 block, 1 space, turn.
    Row 6: 1 space, 1 block, 3 spaces, 3 blocks, 30 spaces, 1 block, 1 space, turn.

Row 7: 1 space, 1 block, 29 spaces, 3 blocks, 4 spaces, 1 block, 1 space, turn.
Row 8: 1 space, 1 block, 5 spaces, 3 blocks, 28 spaces, 1 block, 1 space, turn.
Row 9: 1 space, 1 block, 3 spaces, 2 blocks, 17 spaces, 8 blocks, 2 spaces, 3 blocks, 1 space, 1 block, 1 space, turn.
Row 10: 1 space, 1 block, 2 spaces, 3 blocks, 3 spaces, 7 blocks, 11 spaces, 2 blocks, 2 spaces, 2 blocks, 4 spaces, 1 block, 1 space, turn.
Row 11: 1 space, 1 block, 5 spaces, 2 blocks, 2 spaces, 2 blocks, 10 spaces, 4 blocks, 3 spaces, 4 blocks, 4 spaces, 1 block, 1 space, turn.
Row 12: 1 space, 1 block, 6 spaces, 2 blocks, 2 spaces, 4 blocks, 1 space, 3 blocks, 6 spaces, 2 blocks, 3 spaces, 1 block, 6 spaces, 1 block, 1 space, turn.
Row 13: 1 space, 1 block, 6 spaces, 2 blocks, 3 spaces, 2 blocks, 4 spaces, 4 blocks, 1 space, 6 blocks, 8 spaces, 1 block, 1 space, turn.
Row 14: 1 space, 1 block, 8 spaces, 12 blocks, 2 spaces, 8 blocks, 6 spaces, 1 block, 1 space, turn.
Row 15: 1 space, 1 block, 6 spaces, 24 blocks, 6 spaces, 1 block, 1 space, turn.
Row 16: 1 space, 1 block, 4 spaces, 24 blocks, 8 spaces, 1 block, 1 space, turn.
Row 17: 1 space, 1 block, 9 spaces, 25 blocks, 2 spaces, 1 block, 1 space, turn.
Row 18: 1 space, 1 block, 4 spaces, 23 blocks, 3 spaces, 5 blocks, 1 space, 1 block, 1 space, turn.
Row 19: 1 space, 1 block, 1 space, 6 blocks, 2 spaces, 21 blocks, 1 space, 4 blocks, 1 space, 1 block, 1 space, turn.
Row 20: 1 space, 1 block, 1 space, 8 blocks, 7 spaces, 11 blocks, 1 space, 3 blocks, 2 spaces, 2 blocks, 1 space, 1 block, 1 space, turn.
Row 21: 1 space, 1 block, 1 space, 2 blocks, 4 spaces, 11 blocks, 10 spaces, 5 blocks, 3 spaces, 1 block, 1 space, turn.
Row 22: 1 space, 1 block, 20 spaces, 5 blocks, 8 spaces, 1 block, 2 spaces, 1 block, 1 space, turn.

Rows 23 – 38: 1 space, 1 block, 36 spaces, 1 block, 1 space, turn.
Row 39: 1 space, 38 blocks, 1 space, turn.
Row 40: 40 spaces.

Chart

Chain 125.

Odd rows are worked left to right. Even rows are worked right to left.

Begin rows with ch 5 for the first space.

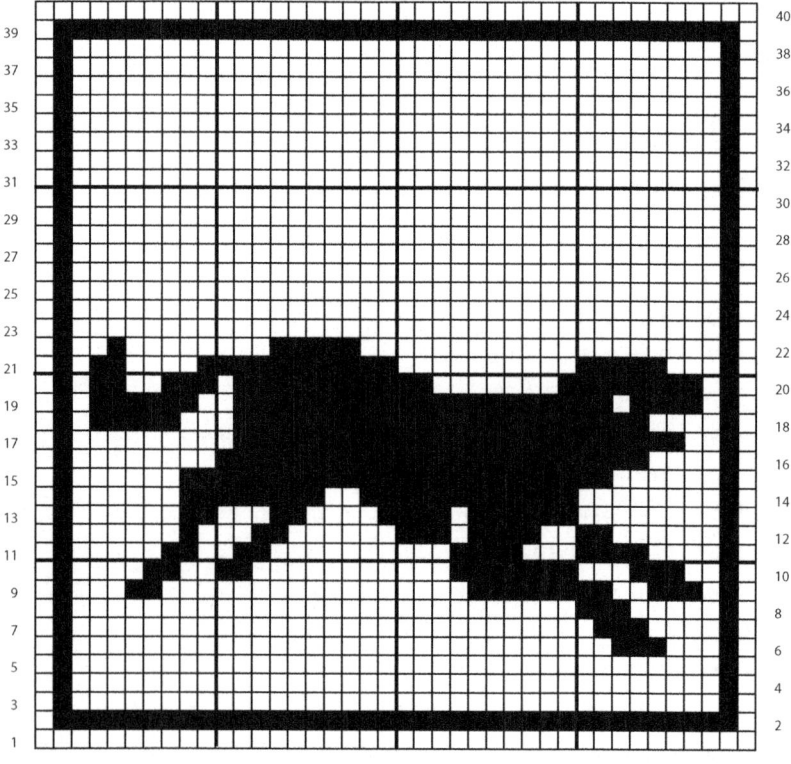

Llama

Written Instructions

Chain 125.
    Row 1: Dc in 8th ch from hook, 39 spaces, turn. 40 squares.
    Row 2: 1 space, 38 blocks, 1 space, turn.
    Row 3: 1 space, 1 block, 36 spaces, 1 block, 1 space, turn.
    Row 4: 1 space, 1 block, 3 spaces, 3 blocks, 5 spaces, 3 blocks, 7 spaces, 3 blocks, 5 spaces, 3 blocks, 4 spaces, 1 block, 1 space, turn.

Row 5: 1 space, 1 block, 5 spaces, 2 blocks, 6 spaces, 2 blocks, 8 spaces, 2 blocks, 6 spaces, 2 blocks, 3 spaces, 1 block, 1 space, turn.

Row 6: 1 space, 1 block, 3 spaces, 1 block, 7 spaces, 1 block, 9 spaces, 1 block, (7 spaces, 1 block) twice, 1 space, turn.

Row 7: 1 space, 1 block, 6 spaces, 1 block, 7 spaces, 1 block, 9 spaces, 2 blocks, 6 spaces, 1 block, 3 spaces, 1 block, 1 space, turn.

Row 8: 1 space, 1 block, 2 spaces, 2 blocks, 6 spaces, 2 blocks, 9 spaces, 2 blocks, 5 spaces, 2 blocks, 6 spaces, 1 block, 1 space, turn.

Row 9: 1 space, 1 block, 6 spaces, 2 blocks, 5 spaces, 2 blocks, 10 spaces, 2 blocks, 5 spaces, 2 blocks, 2 spaces, 1 block, 1 space, turn.

Row 10: 1 space, 1 block, 2 spaces, 2 blocks, 5 spaces, 2 blocks, 10 spaces, 2 blocks, 5 spaces, 2 blocks, 6 spaces, 1 block, 1 space, turn.

Row 11: 1 space, 1 block, 7 spaces, 2 blocks, 4 spaces, 2 blocks, 11 spaces, 2 blocks, 4 spaces, 2 blocks, 2 spaces, 1 block, 1 space, turn.

Row 12: 1 space, 1 block, 2 spaces, 2 blocks, 4 spaces, 2 blocks, 11 spaces, 2 blocks, 4 spaces, 2 blocks, 7 spaces, 1 block, 1 space, turn.

Row 13: 1 space, 1 block, 7 spaces, 2 blocks, 4 spaces, 2 blocks, 11 spaces, (3 blocks, 2 spaces) twice, 1 block, 1 space, turn.

Row 14: 1 space, 1 block, 1 space, 4 blocks, 2 spaces, 3 blocks, 11 spaces, 3 blocks, 2 spaces, 3 blocks, 7 spaces, 1 block, 1 space, turn.

Row 15: 1 space, 1 block, 8 spaces, 3 blocks, 1 space, 3 blocks, 10 spaces, 3 blocks, 3 spaces, 4 blocks, 1 space, 1 block, 1 space, turn.

Row 16: 1 space, 1 block, 2 spaces, 4 blocks, 2 spaces, 3 blocks, 10 spaces, 7 blocks, 8 spaces, 1 block, 1 space, turn.

Row 17: 1 space, 1 block, 7 spaces, 11 blocks, 6 spaces, 4 blocks, 1 space, 4 blocks, 3 spaces, 1 block, 1 space, turn.

Row 18: (1 space, 1 block) twice, 2 spaces, 4 blocks, 1 space, 4 blocks, 3 spaces, 15 blocks, 5 spaces, 1 block, 1 space, turn.

Row 19: 1 space, 1 block, 4 spaces, 18 blocks, 1 space, 9 blocks, 2 spaces, (1 block, 1 space) twice, turn.

Row 20: (1 space, 1 block) twice, 2 spaces, 29 blocks, 3 spaces, 1 block, 1 space, turn.

Row 21: 1 space, 1 block, 3 spaces, 29 blocks, 2 spaces, (1 block, 1 space) twice, turn.

Row 22: (1 space, 1 block) twice, 2 spaces, 29 blocks, 3 spaces, 1 block, 1 space, turn.

Row 23: 1 space, 1 block, 3 spaces, 5 blocks, 1 space, 23 blocks, 1 space, 1 block, 2 spaces, 1 block, 1 space, turn.

Row 24: 1 space, 1 block, 3 spaces, 23 blocks, 2 spaces, 5 blocks, 3 spaces, 1 block, 1 space, turn.

Row 25: 1 space, 1 block, 4 spaces, 5 blocks, 2 spaces, 21 blocks, 4 spaces, 1 block, 1 space, turn.

Row 26: 1 space, 1 block, 4 spaces, 20 blocks, 3 spaces, 4 blocks, 5 spaces, 1 block, 1 space, turn.

Row 27: 1 space, 1 block, 6 spaces, 3 blocks, 4 spaces, 17 blocks, 6 spaces, 1 block, 1 space, turn.

Row 28: 1 space, 1 block, 7 spaces, 15 blocks, 4 spaces, 3 blocks, 7 spaces, 1 block, 1 space, turn.

Row 29: 1 space, 1 block, 7 spaces, 3 blocks, 5 spaces, 13 blocks, 8 spaces, 1 block, 1 space, turn.

Row 30: 1 space, 1 block, 10 spaces, 10 blocks, 6 spaces, 3 blocks, 7 spaces, 1 block, 1 space, turn.

Row 31: 1 space, 1 block, 6 spaces, 4 blocks, 7 spaces, 8 blocks, 11 spaces, 1 block, 1 space, turn.

Row 32: 1 space, 1 block, 12 spaces, 6 blocks, 8 spaces, 9 blocks, 1 space, 1 block, 1 space, turn.

Row 33: (1 space, 1 block) twice, 1 space, 8 blocks, 25 spaces, 1 block, 1 space, turn.

Row 34: 1 space, 1 block, 25 spaces, 3 blocks, 1 space, 5 blocks, 2 spaces, 1 block, 1 space, turn.

Row 35: 1 space, 1 block, 4 spaces, 7 blocks, 25 spaces, 1 block, 1 space, turn.

Row 36: 1 space, 1 block, 25 spaces, 1 block, 1 space, 1 block, 8 spaces, 1 block, 1 space, turn.

Row 37: 1 space, 1 block, 7 spaces, 1 block, 2 spaces, 1 block, 25 spaces, 1 block, 1 space, turn.

Row 38: 1 space, 1 block, 36 spaces, 1 block, 1 space, turn.

Row 39: 1 space, 38 blocks, 1 space, turn.

Row 40: 40 spaces.

Chart

Chain 125.

Odd rows are worked left to right. Even rows are worked right to left.

Begin rows with ch 5 for the first space.

Camel

Written Instructions

Chain 125.

Row 1: Dc in 8th ch from hook, 39 spaces, turn. 40 squares.
Row 2: 1 space, 38 blocks, 1 space, turn.
Rows 3 – 4: 1 space, 1 block, 36 spaces, 1 block, 1 space, turn.
Row 5: 1 space, 1 block, 4 spaces, 3 blocks, 3 spaces, 3 blocks, (6 spaces, 3 blocks) twice, 5 spaces, 1 block, 1 space, turn.
Rows 6, 8: 1 space, 1 block, 5 spaces, (2 blocks, 7 spaces) twice, 2 blocks, 4 spaces, 2 blocks, 5 spaces, 1 block, 1 space, turn.

Rows 7, 9: 1 space, 1 block, 5 spaces, 2 blocks, 4 spaces, 2 blocks, (7 spaces, 2 blocks) twice, 5 spaces, 1 block, 1 space, turn.

Row 10: 1 space, 1 block, 5 spaces, (2 blocks, 7 spaces) twice, 3 blocks, 2 spaces, 3 blocks, 5 spaces, 1 block, 1 space, turn.

Row 11: 1 space, 1 block, 6 spaces, 2 blocks, 2 spaces, 3 blocks, 8 spaces, 2 blocks, 6 spaces, 2 blocks, 5 spaces, 1 block, 1 space, turn.

Row 12: 1 space, 1 block, 5 spaces, 2 blocks, 5 spaces, 3 blocks, 8 spaces, 3 blocks, 1 space, 3 blocks, 6 spaces, 1 block, 1 space, turn.

Row 13: 1 space, 1 block, 6 spaces, 3 blocks, 1 space, 3 blocks, 8 spaces, 3 blocks, 5 spaces, 3 blocks, 4 spaces, 1 block, 1 space, turn.

Row 14: 1 space, 1 block, 4 spaces, 4 blocks, 3 spaces, 3 blocks, 8 spaces, 4 blocks, 1 space, 4 blocks, 5 spaces, 1 block, 1 space, turn.

Row 15: 1 space, 1 block, 5 spaces, 4 blocks, 1 space, 4 blocks, 8 spaces, 3 blocks, 2 spaces, 4 blocks, 5 spaces, 1 block, 1 space, turn.

Row 16: 1 space, 1 block, 6 spaces, 4 blocks, 2 spaces, 3 blocks, 7 spaces, 4 blocks, 1 space, 4 blocks, 5 spaces, 1 block, 1 space, turn.

Row 17: 1 space, 1 block, 5 spaces, 12 blocks, 3 spaces, 4 blocks, 1 space, 5 blocks, 4 spaces, (1 block, 1 space) twice, turn.

Row 18: 1 space, 1 block, 2 spaces, 1 block, 4 spaces, 24 blocks, 5 spaces, 1 block, 1 space, turn.

Row 19: 1 space, 1 block, 5 spaces, 24 blocks, (3 spaces, 1 block) twice, 1 space, turn.

Row 20: 1 space, 1 block, 4 spaces, 1 block, 2 spaces, 24 blocks, 5 spaces, 1 block, 1 space, turn.

Row 21: 1 space, 1 block, 5 spaces, 24 blocks, 1 space, 1 block, 5 spaces, 1 block, 1 space, turn.

Row 22: 1 space, 1 block, 6 spaces, 25 blocks, 5 spaces, 1 block, 1 space, turn.

Row 23: 1 space, 1 block, 5 spaces, 24 blocks, 7 spaces, 1 block, 1 space, turn.

Row 24: 1 space, 1 block, 8 spaces, 23 blocks, 5 spaces, 1 block, 1 space, turn.

Row 25: 1 space, 1 block, 5 spaces, 4 blocks, 1 space, 17 blocks, 9 spaces, 1 block, 1 space, turn.

Row 26: 1 space, 1 block, 10 spaces, 15 blocks, 2 spaces, 3 blocks, 6 spaces, 1 block, 1 space, turn.

Row 27: 1 space, 1 block, 6 spaces, 3 blocks, 3 spaces, 13 blocks, 11 spaces, 1 block, 1 space, turn.

Row 28: 1 space, 1 block, 12 spaces, 6 blocks, 1 space, 5 blocks, 3 spaces, 3 blocks, 6 spaces, 1 block, 1 space, turn.

Row 29: 1 space, 1 block, 7 spaces, (3 blocks, 3 spaces) twice, 4 blocks, 13 spaces, 1 block, 1 space, turn.

Row 30: 1 space, 1 block, 26 spaces, 3 blocks, 7 spaces, 1 block, 1 space, turn.

Row 31: 1 space, 1 block, 8 spaces, 3 blocks, 25 spaces, 1 block, 1 space, turn.

Row 32: 1 space, 1 block, 24 spaces, 9 blocks, 3 spaces, 1 block, 1 space, turn.

Row 33: 1 space, 1 block, 3 spaces, 5 blocks, 1 space, 3 blocks, 24 spaces, 1 block, 1 space, turn.

Row 34: 1 space, 1 block, 24 spaces, 8 blocks, 4 spaces, 1 block, 1 space, turn.

Row 35: 1 space, 1 block, 6 spaces, 5 blocks, 25 spaces, 1 block, 1 space, turn.

Row 36: 1 space, 1 block, 25 spaces, 1 block, 1 space, 1 block, 8 spaces, 1 block, 1 space, turn.

Rows 37 – 38: 1 space, 1 block, 36 spaces, 1 block, 1 space, turn.

Row 39: 1 space, 38 blocks, 1 space, turn.

Row 40: 40 spaces.

Chart

Chain 125.

Odd rows are worked left to right. Even rows are worked right to left.

Begin rows with ch 5 for the first space.

Squirrel

Written Instructions

Chain 125.

Row 1: Dc in 8th ch from hook, 39 spaces, turn. 40 squares.
Row 2: 1 space, 38 blocks, 1 space, turn.
Row 3: 1 space, 1 block, 36 spaces, 1 block, 1 space, turn.
Row 4: 1 space, 1 block, 23 spaces, 7 blocks, 6 spaces, 1 block, 1 space, turn.
Row 5: 1 space, 1 block, 36 spaces, 1 block, 1 space, turn.
Row 6: 1 space, 1 block, 9 spaces, 5 blocks, 22 spaces, 1 block, 1 space, turn.
Row 7: 1 space, 1 block, 8 spaces, 4 blocks, 5 spaces, 1 block, 1 space, 5 blocks, 7 spaces, 4 blocks, 1 space, 1 block, 1 space, turn.
Row 8: 1 space, 1 block, 7 spaces, 11 blocks, 1 space, 2 blocks, 15 spaces, 1 block, 1 space, turn.
Row 9: 1 space, 1 block, 15 spaces, 10 blocks, 11 spaces, 1 block, 1 space, turn.
Row 10: 1 space, 1 block, 10 spaces, 12 blocks, 14 spaces, 1 block, 1 space, turn.
Row 11: 1 space, 1 block, 14 spaces, 2 blocks, 1 space, 3 blocks, 1 space, 6 blocks, 9 spaces, 1 block, 1 space, turn.
Row 12: 1 space, 1 block, 9 spaces, 6 blocks, 1 space, 3 blocks, 1 space, 2 blocks, 14 spaces, 1 block, 1 space, turn.
Row 13: 1 space, 1 block, 13 spaces, 2 blocks, 1 space, 5 blocks, 1 space, 5 blocks, 9 spaces, 1 block, 1 space, turn.
Row 14: 1 space, 1 block, 10 spaces, 1 block, 3 spaces, 6 blocks, 1 space, 3 blocks, 12 spaces, 1 block, 1 space, turn.

Row 15: 1 space, 1 block, 12 spaces, 3 blocks, (1 space, 1 block) twice, 2 spaces, 5 blocks, 10 spaces, 1 block, 1 space, turn.

Row 16: 1 space, 1 block, 9 spaces, 3 blocks, 1 space, 7 blocks, 1 space, 3 blocks, 12 spaces, 1 block, 1 space, turn.

Row 17: 1 space, 1 block, 12 spaces, 4 blocks, 1 space, 6 blocks, 1 space, 3 blocks, 9 spaces, 1 block, 1 space, turn.

Row 18: 1 space, 1 block, 9 spaces, 2 blocks, 1 space, 7 blocks, 1 space, 4 blocks, 12 spaces, 1 block, 1 space, turn.

Row 19: 1 space, 1 block, 12 spaces, 4 blocks, 1 space, 7 blocks, 1 space, 2 blocks, 9 spaces, 1 block, 1 space, turn.

Row 20: 1 space, 1 block, 8 spaces, 2 blocks, 1 space, 7 blocks, 1 space, 4 blocks, 13 spaces, 1 block, 1 space, turn.

Row 21: 1 space, 1 block, 13 spaces, 4 blocks, 1 space, 7 blocks, 1 space, 2 blocks, 8 spaces, 1 block, 1 space, turn.

Row 22: 1 space, 1 block, 2 spaces, 2 blocks, 2 spaces, 11 blocks, 1 space, 6 blocks, 12 spaces, 1 block, 1 space, turn.

Row 23: 1 space, 1 block, 11 spaces, 7 blocks, 2 spaces, 15 blocks, 1 space, 1 block, 1 space, turn.

Row 24: (1 space, 1 block) twice, 1 space, 2 blocks, 2 spaces, 1 block, 1 space, 6 blocks, 3 spaces, 8 blocks, 10 spaces, 1 block, 1 space, turn.

Row 25: 1 space, 1 block, 5 spaces, 14 blocks, 3 spaces, 9 blocks, 1 space, 2 blocks, 2 spaces, 1 block, 1 space, turn.

Row 26: 1 space, 1 block, 3 spaces, 10 blocks, 4 spaces, 15 blocks, 4 spaces, 1 block, 1 space, turn.

Row 27: 1 space, 1 block, 3 spaces, 16 blocks, 5 spaces, 9 blocks, 3 spaces, 1 block, 1 space, turn.

Row 28: 1 space, 1 block, 4 spaces, 1 block, 1 space, 6 blocks, 6 spaces, 14 blocks, 4 spaces, 1 block, 1 space, turn.

Row 29: 1 space, 1 block, 2 spaces, 16 blocks, 7 spaces, 7 blocks, 4 spaces, 1 block, 1 space, turn.

Row 30: 1 space, 1 block, 5 spaces, 5 blocks, 8 spaces, 15 blocks, 3 spaces, 1 block, 1 space, turn.

Row 31: 1 space, 1 block, 4 spaces, 13 blocks, 10 spaces, 3 blocks, 6 spaces, 1 block, 1 space, turn.

Row 32: 1 space, 1 block, 7 spaces, 1 block, 1 space, 1 block, 10 spaces, 11 blocks, 5 spaces, 1 block, 1 space, turn.

Row 33: 1 space, 1 block, 7 spaces, 8 blocks, 21 spaces, 1 block, 1 space, turn.

Row 34: 1 space, 1 block, 22 spaces, 6 blocks, 8 spaces, 1 block, 1 space, turn.

Rows 35 – 38: 1 space, 1 block, 36 spaces, 1 block, 1 space, turn.

Row 39: 1 space, 38 blocks, 1 space, turn.

Row 40: 40 spaces.

Chart

Chain 125.

Odd rows are worked left to right. Even rows are worked right to left.

Begin rows with ch 5 for the first space.

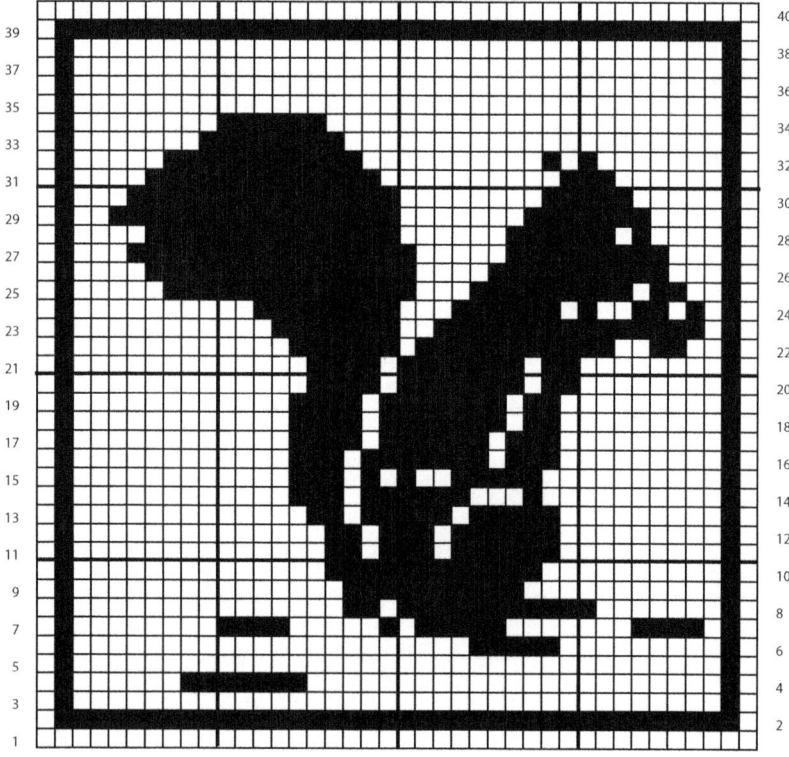

Horse

Written Instructions

Chain 125.
Row 1: Dc in 8th ch from hook, 39 spaces, turn. 40 squares.
Row 2: 1 space, 38 blocks, 1 space, turn.
Rows 3 – 4: 1 space, 1 block, 36 spaces, 1 block, 1 space, turn.
Row 5: 1 space, 1 block, 4 spaces, 2 blocks, 1 space, 8 blocks, 1 space, 2 blocks, 1 space, 1 block, 2 spaces, 1 block, 1 space, 11 blocks, 1 space, 1 block, 1 space, turn.
Row 6: 1 space, 1 block, 14 spaces, 1 block, 4 spaces, 1 block, 11 spaces, 1 block, 4 spaces, 1 block, 1 space, turn.
Row 7: 1 space, 1 block, 4 spaces, 1 block, 11 spaces, 1 block, 4 spaces, 1 block, 9 spaces, 1 block, 4 spaces, 1 block, 1 space, turn.
Row 8: 1 space, 1 block, 3 spaces, 1 block, 10 spaces, 1 block, 4 spaces, 2 blocks, 9 spaces, 2 blocks, 4 spaces, 1 block, 1 space, turn.
Row 9: 1 space, 1 block, 4 spaces, 2 blocks, 8 spaces, 2 blocks, 5 spaces, 1 block, 10 spaces, 1 block, 3 spaces, 1 block, 1 space, turn.
Row 10: 1 space, 1 block, 3 spaces, 1 block, 9 spaces, 2 blocks, 6 spaces, 1 block, 7 spaces, 2 blocks, 5 spaces, 1 block, 1 space, turn.
Row 11: 1 space, 1 block, 6 spaces, 2 blocks, 5 spaces, 2 blocks, 6 spaces, 2 blocks, 9 spaces, 1 block, 3 spaces, 1 block, 1 space, turn.
Row 12: 1 space, 1 block, 3 spaces, 1 block, (8 spaces, 2 blocks) twice, 2 spaces, 4 blocks, 6 spaces, 1 block, 1 space, turn.
Row 13: 1 space, 1 block, 7 spaces, 3 blocks, 1 space, 3 blocks, 9 spaces, 2 blocks, 3 spaces, 4 blocks, 4 spaces, 1 block, 1 space, turn.
Row 14: 1 space, 1 block, 6 spaces, 7 blocks, 5 spaces, 11 blocks, 4 spaces, 2 blocks, 1 space, 1 block, 1 space, turn.

Row 15: 1 space, 1 block, 2 spaces, 2 blocks, 3 spaces, 8 blocks 3 spaces, 11 blocks, 7 spaces, 1 block, 1 space, turn.

Row 16: 1 space, 1 block, 7 spaces, 21 blocks, 4 spaces, 2 blocks, 2 spaces, 1 block, 1 space, turn.

Row 17: 1 space, 1 block, 2 spaces, 3 blocks, 3 spaces, 21 blocks, 7 spaces, 1 block, 1 space, turn.

Row 18: 1 space, 1 block, 6 spaces, 24 blocks, 1 space, 2 blocks, 3 spaces, 1 block, 1 space, turn.

Row 19: 1 space, 1 block, 4 spaces, 2 blocks, 2 spaces, 22 blocks, 2 spaces, 2 blocks, 2 spaces, 1 block, 1 space, turn.

Row 20: 1 space, 1 block, 2 spaces, 3 blocks, 1 space, 22 blocks, 2 spaces, 2 blocks, 4 spaces, 1 block, 1 space, turn.

Row 21: 1 space, 1 block, 6 spaces, 2 blocks, 1 space, 21 blocks, 1 space, 4 blocks, 1 space, 1 block, 1 space, turn.

Row 22: 1 space, 1 block, 1 space, 27 blocks, 8 spaces, 1 block, 1 space, turn.

Row 23: 1 space, 1 block, 10 spaces, 7 blocks, 4 spaces, 14 blocks, 1 space, 1 block, 1 space, turn.

Row 24: 1 space, 1 block, 1 space, 13 blocks, 23 spaces, 1 block, 1 space, turn.

Row 25: 1 space, 1 block, 25 spaces, 6 blocks, 1 space, 3 blocks, 1 space, 1 block, 1 space, turn.

Row 26: 1 space, 1 block, 1 space, 3 blocks, 2 spaces, 4 blocks, 26 spaces, 1 block, 1 space, turn.

Row 27: 1 space, 1 block, 27 spaces, 7 blocks, 2 spaces, 1 block, 1 space, turn.

Row 28: 1 space, 1 block, 3 spaces, 5 blocks, 28 spaces, 1 block, 1 space, turn.

Row 29: 1 space, 1 block, 29 spaces, 3 blocks, 1 space, 1 block, 2 spaces, 1 block, 1 space, turn.

Row 30: 1 space, 1 block, (2 spaces, 1 block) twice, 14 spaces, 2 blocks, 14 spaces, 1 block, 1 space, turn.

Row 31: 1 space, 1 block, 13 spaces, 4 blocks, 13 spaces, 1 block, 5 spaces, 1 block, 1 space, turn.

Row 32: 1 space, 1 block, 20 spaces, 2 blocks, 14 spaces, 1 block, 1 space, turn.

Rows 33 – 38: 1 space, 1 block, 36 spaces, 1 block, 1 space, turn.

Row 39: 1 space, 38 blocks, 1 space, turn.

Row 40: 40 spaces.

Chart

Chain 125.

Odd rows are worked left to right. Even rows are worked right to left.

Begin rows with ch 5 for the first space.

Goat

Written Instructions

Chain 125.

Row 1: Dc in 8th ch from hook, 39 spaces, turn. 40 squares.

Row 2: 1 space, 38 blocks, 1 space, turn.

Row 3: 1 space, 1 block, 36 spaces, 1 block, 1 space, turn.

Row 4: 1 space, 1 block, 15 spaces, 2 blocks, 11 spaces, 2 blocks, 3 spaces, 2 blocks, 1 space, 1 block, 1 space, turn.

Row 5: 1 space, 1 block, 1 space, 2 blocks, 3 spaces, 2 blocks, 11 spaces, 2 blocks, 1 space, 1 block, 13 spaces, 1 block, 1 space, turn.

Row 6: 1 space, 1 block, 13 spaces, 2 blocks, 1 space, 1 block, 12 spaces, 1 block, 4 spaces, (1 block, 1 space) twice, turn.

Row 7: (1 space, 1 block) twice, 4 spaces, 1 block, 12 spaces, 1 block, 1 space, 1 block, 14 spaces, 1 block, 1 space, turn.

Row 8: 1 space, 1 block, 14 spaces, 1 block, 1 space, 2 blocks, 11 spaces, 2 blocks, 3 spaces, (1 block, 1 space) twice, turn.

Row 9: 1 space, 1 block, 1 space, 2 blocks, 2 spaces, 2 blocks, 11 spaces, 2 blocks, 1 space, 1 block, 14 spaces, 1 block, 1 space, turn.

Row 10: 1 space, 1 block, 14 spaces, 1 block, 1 space, 5 blocks, 6 spaces, 1 block, 1 space, 2 blocks, 1 space, 3 blocks, 1 space, 1 block, 1 space, turn.

Row 11: 1 space, 1 block, 2 spaces, 8 blocks, 3 spaces, 10 blocks, 13 spaces, 1 block, 1 space, turn.

Row 12: 1 space, 1 block, 13 spaces, 10 blocks, 2 spaces, 8 blocks, 3 spaces, 1 block, 1 space, turn.

Row 13: 1 space, 1 block, 2 spaces, 16 blocks, 2 spaces, 3 blocks, 13 spaces, 1 block, 1 space, turn.

Row 14: 1 space, 1 block, 12 spaces, 15 blocks, 1 space, 6 blocks, 2 spaces, 1 block, 1 space, turn.

Row 15: 1 space, 1 block, 2 spaces, 6 blocks, 1 space, 16 blocks, 11 spaces, 1 block, 1 space, turn.

Row 16: 1 space, 1 block, 11 spaces, 23 blocks, 2 spaces, 1 block, 1 space, turn.

Row 17: 1 space, 1 block, 2 spaces, 23 blocks, 1 space, 1 block, 9 spaces, 1 block, 1 space, turn.

Row 18: 1 space, 1 block, 9 spaces, 25 blocks, 2 spaces, 1 block, 1 space, turn.

Row 19: 1 space, 1 block, 3 spaces, 24 blocks, 9 spaces, 1 block, 1 space, turn.

Row 20: 1 space, 1 block, 4 spaces, 1 block, 4 spaces, 24 blocks, 3 spaces, 1 block, 1 space, turn.

Row 21: 1 space, 1 block, 2 spaces, 26 blocks, 3 spaces, 1 block, 4 spaces, 1 block, 1 space, turn.

Row 22: 1 space, 1 block, 3 spaces, 2 blocks, 3 spaces, 24 blocks, 1 space, 2 blocks, 1 space, 1 block, 1 space, turn.

Row 23: 1 space, 1 block, 1 space, 2 blocks, 1 space, 24 blocks, 1 space, 1 block, 1 space, 3 blocks, 2 spaces, 1 block, 1 space, turn.

Row 24: 1 space, 1 block, 1 space, 14 blocks, 10 spaces, 6 blocks, 3 spaces, (1 block, 1 space) twice, turn.

Row 25: 1 space, 1 block, 21 spaces, 14 blocks, 1 space, 1 block, 1 space, turn.

Row 26: 1 space, 1 block, 1 space, 12 spaces, 23 spaces, 1 block, 1 space, turn.

Row 27: 1 space, 1 block, 24 spaces, 10 blocks, 2 spaces, 1 block, 1 space, turn.

Row 28: 1 space, 1 block, 2 spaces, 2 blocks, 1 space, 5 blocks, 26 spaces, 1 block, 1 space, turn.

Row 29: 1 space, 1 block, 25 spaces, 9 blocks, 2 spaces, 1 block, 1 space, turn.

Row 30: 1 space, 1 block, 2 spaces, 9 blocks, 25 spaces, 1 block, 1 space, turn.

Row 31: 1 space, 1 block, 26 spaces, 6 blocks, 1 space, 1 block, 2 spaces, 1 block, 1 space, turn.

Row 32: 1 space, 1 block, 6 spaces, 2 blocks, 1 space, 4 blocks, 23 spaces, 1 block, 1 space, turn.

Row 33: 1 space, 1 block, 21 spaces, 5 blocks, 2 spaces, 1 block, 7 spaces, 1 block, 1 space, turn.

Row 34: 1 space, 1 block, (7 spaces, 1 block) twice, 20 spaces, 1 block, 1 space, turn.

Rows 35 – 38: 1 space, 1 block, 36 spaces, 1 block, 1 space, turn.

Row 39: 1 space, 38 blocks, 1 space, turn.

Row 40: 40 spaces.

Chart

Chain 125.

Odd rows are worked left to right. Even rows are worked right to left.

Begin rows with ch 5 for the first space.

Rabbit

Written Instructions

Chain 125.
   Row 1: Dc in 8th ch from hook, 39 spaces, turn. 40 squares.
   Row 2: 1 space, 38 blocks, 1 space, turn.
   Rows 3 – 4: 1 space, 1 block, 36 spaces, 1 block, 1 space, turn.
   Row 5: 1 space, 1 block, 2 spaces, 8 blocks, 8 spaces, 8 blocks, 10 spaces, 1 block, 1 space, turn.
   Row 6: 1 space, 1 block, 36 spaces, 1 block, 1 space, turn.
   Row 7: 1 space, 1 block, 11 spaces, 6 blocks, 9 spaces, 3 blocks, 7 spaces, 1 block, 1 space, turn.
   Row 8: 1 space, 1 block, 6 spaces, 3 blocks, 3 spaces, 7 blocks, 1 space, 12 blocks, 4 spaces, 1 block, 1 space, turn.
   Row 9: 1 space, 1 block, 4 spaces, 12 blocks, 1 space, 6 blocks, 6 spaces, 2 blocks, 5 spaces, 1 block, 1 space, turn.
   Row 10: 1 space, 1 block, 4 spaces, 1 block, 9 spaces, 4 blocks, 1 space, 12 blocks, 5 spaces, 1 block, 1 space, turn.
   Row 11: 1 space, 1 block, 5 spaces, 12 blocks, 1 space, 5 blocks, 13 spaces, 1 block, 1 space, turn.
   Row 12: 1 space, 1 block, 12 spaces, 6 blocks, 1 space, 12 blocks, 5 spaces, 1 block, 1 space, turn.
   Row 13: 1 space, 1 block, 5 spaces, 11 blocks, 1 space, 8 blocks, 11 spaces, 1 block, 1 space, turn.
   Row 14: 1 space, 1 block, 10 spaces, 9 blocks, 1 space, 10 blocks, 6 spaces, 1 block, 1 space, turn.
   Row 15: 1 space, 1 block, 7 spaces, 4 blocks, 1 space, 3 blocks, 1 space, 10 blocks, 10 spaces, 1 block, 1 space, turn.

Row 16: 1 space, 1 block, 6 spaces, 4 blocks, 1 space, 10 blocks, 3 spaces, 4 blocks, 8 spaces, 1 block, 1 space, turn.

Row 17: 1 space, 1 block, 9 spaces, 15 blocks, 1 space, 5 blocks, 6 spaces, 1 block, 1 space, turn.

Row 18: 1 space, 1 block, 6 spaces, 6 blocks, 1 space, 11 blocks, 12 spaces, 1 block, 1 space, turn.

Row 19: 1 space, 1 block, 13 spaces, 5 blocks, 3 spaces, 5 blocks, 1 space, 2 blocks, 7 spaces, 1 block, 1 space, turn.

Row 20: 1 space, 1 block, 8 spaces, 5 blocks, 23 spaces, 1 block, 1 space, turn.

Row 21: 1 space, 1 block, 23 spaces, 5 blocks, 8 spaces, 1 block, 1 space, turn.

Row 22: 1 space, 1 block, 9 spaces, 8 blocks, 19 spaces, 1 block, 1 space, turn.

Row 23: 1 space, 1 block, 18 spaces, 3 blocks, 1 space, 3 blocks, 11 spaces, 1 block, 1 space, turn.

Row 24: 1 space, 1 block, 12 spaces, 3 blocks, 1 space, 3 blocks, 17 spaces, 1 block, 1 space, turn.

Row 25: 1 space, 1 block, 16 spaces, 2 blocks, 2 spaces, 3 blocks, 13 spaces, 1 block, 1 space, turn.

Row 26: 1 space, 1 block, 14 spaces, 3 blocks, 2 spaces, 2 blocks, 15 spaces, 1 block, 1 space, turn.

Row 27: 1 space, 1 block, 15 spaces, 1 block, 2 spaces, 3 blocks, 15 spaces, 1 block, 1 space, turn.

Row 28: 1 space, 1 block, 16 spaces, 2 blocks, 18 spaces, 1 block, 1 space, turn.

Row 29: 1 space, 1 block, 17 spaces, 1 block, 18 spaces, 1 block, 1 space, turn.

Rows 30 – 38: 1 space, 1 block, 36 spaces, 1 block, 1 space, turn.
Row 39: 1 space, 38 blocks, 1 space, turn.
Row 40: 40 spaces.

Chart

Chain 125.

Odd rows are worked left to right. Even rows are worked right to left.

Begin rows with ch 5 for the first space.

Plain Block

Written Instructions

Chain 125.
    Row 1: Dc in 8th ch from hook, 39 spaces, turn. 40 squares.
    Row 2: 1 space, 38 blocks, 1 space, turn.
    Rows 3–38: 1 space, 1 block, 36 spaces, 1 block, 1 space, turn.
    Row 39: 1 space, 38 blocks, 1 space, turn.
    Row 40: 40 spaces.

Chart

Chain 125.

Odd rows are worked left to right. Even rows are worked right to left.

Begin rows with ch 5 for the first space.

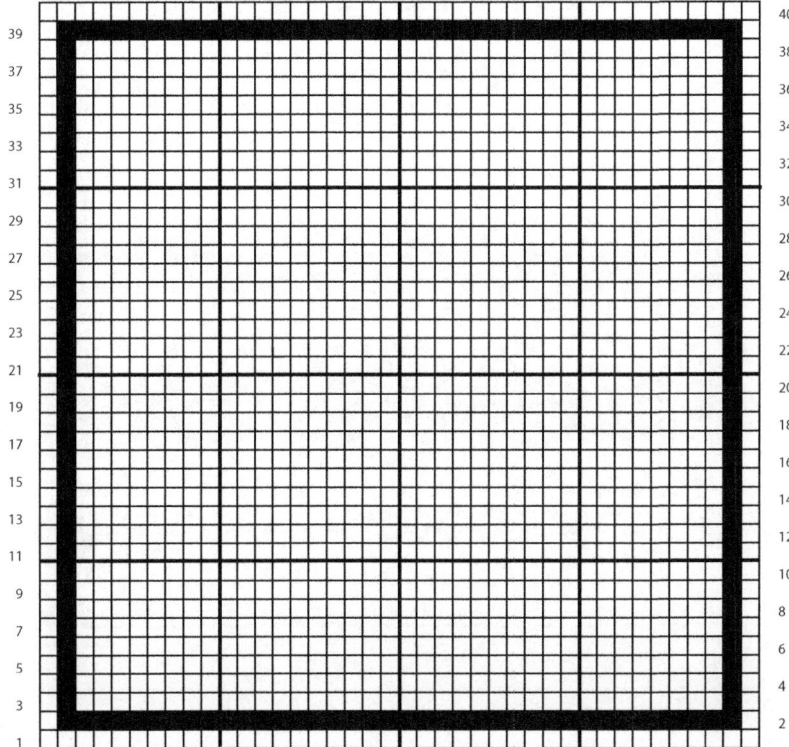

Checkered Block

Written Instructions

Chain 125.

Row 1: Dc in 8th ch from hook, 39 spaces, turn. 40 squares.

Row 2: 1 space, 38 blocks, 1 space, turn.

Row 3: 1 space, 1 block, 36 spaces, 1 block, 1 space, turn.

Rows 4 – 37: (1 space, 1 block) 18 times, 2 spaces, 1 block, 1 space, turn.

Row 38: 1 space, 1 block, 36 spaces, 1 block, 1 space, turn.

Row 39: 1 space, 38 blocks, 1 space, turn.
Row 40: 40 spaces.

Chart

Chain 125.

Odd rows are worked left to right. Even rows are worked right to left.

Begin rows with ch 5 for the first space.

Zoo Border

If you need a straight border for a different project, start at Row 53, with a foundation of 50 chain.

Increases are made by adding foundation chains at the beginning of a row.

Decreases are made by slip stitching over squares at the beginning of a row.

Corner: after a 1-space decrease at the beginning of Row 24, the border is worked straight to the end. Then the work is turned. The next row is done along the edge of the previous rows, and the border is worked straight to the next corner. See chart for clarification.

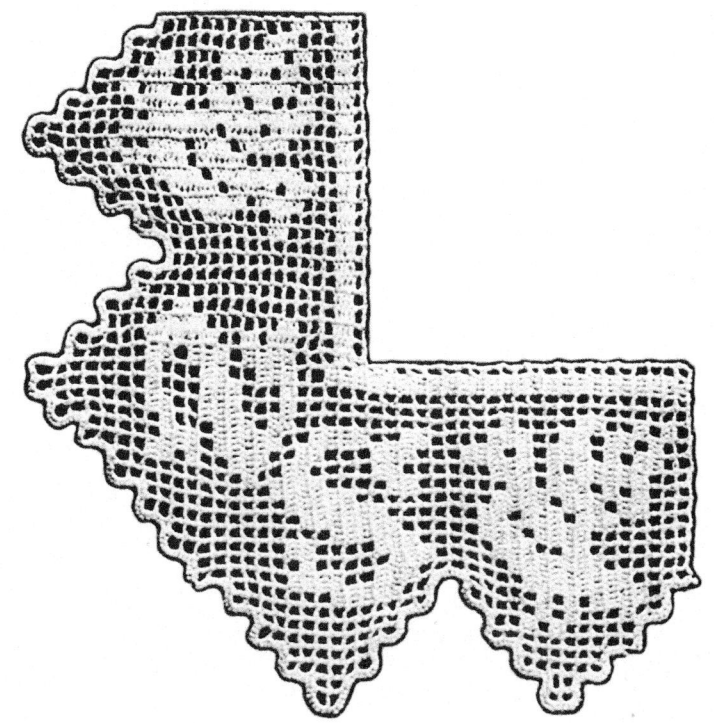

Flying Goose

Starting near one side of corner, chain 50.

Row 1: Dc 8th stitch from hook, 12 more spaces, 1 block, 1 space, turn. 15 squares.

Row 2: 1 space, 1 block, 2 spaces, 1 block, 10 spaces, turn.

Row 3: Ch 10, dc in 8th stitch from hook, ch 2, dc in last dc of preceding row, 8 spaces, 2 blocks, 3 spaces, 1 block, 1 space, turn. 17 squares.

Row 4: 1 space, 1 block, 2 spaces, 1 block, 1 space, 4 blocks, 5 spaces, 1 block, 1 space, turn.

Row 5: Ch 10, dc in 8th stitch from hook, ch 2, dc in last dc of preceding row, 3 blocks, 4 spaces, 1 block, (1 space, 1 block) twice, 3 spaces, 1 block, 1 space, turn. 19 squares.

Row 6: 1 space, 1 block, 3 spaces, 4 blocks, 1 space, 1 block, 3 spaces, 2 blocks, 3 spaces, turn.

Row 7: Ch 10, dc in 8th stitch from hook, ch 2, dc in last dc of preceding row, 3 spaces, 3 blocks, 2 spaces, 2 blocks, 1 space, (1 block, 2 spaces) twice, 1 block, 1 space, turn. 21 squares.

Row 8: 1 space, 1 block, 2 spaces, 11 blocks, 6 spaces, turn.

Row 9: Ch 10, dc in 8th stitch from hook, ch 2, dc in last dc of preceding row, 4 spaces, 6 blocks, (1 space, 2 blocks) twice, 3 spaces, 1 block, 1 space, turn. 23 squares.

Row 10: 1 space, 1 block, 4 spaces, 3 blocks, (1 space, 2 blocks) twice, 2 spaces, 1 block, 5 spaces, turn.

Row 11: Slip over 2 spaces, 4 spaces, 4 blocks, 1 space, 3 blocks, 7 spaces, 1 block, 1 space, turn. 21 squares.

Row 12: 1 space, 1 block, 3 spaces, 6 blocks, 1 space, 3 blocks, 2 spaces, 1 block, 3 spaces, turn.

Row 13: Slip over 2 spaces, 5 spaces, (3 blocks, 1 space) twice, 2 blocks, 2 spaces, 1 block, 1 space, turn. 19 squares.

Row 14: 1 space, 1 block, 3 spaces, 3 blocks, 1 space, 4 blocks, 6 spaces, turn.

Row 15: Slip over 2 spaces, 5 spaces, 2 blocks, 3 spaces, 1 block, 4 spaces, 1 block, 1 space, turn. 17 squares.

Row 16: 1 space, 1 block, 4 spaces, 1 block, 10 spaces, turn.

Row 17: Slip over 2 spaces, 13 spaces, 1 block, 1 space, turn. 15 squares.

Snake and Corner

Row 18: 1 space, 1 block, 13 spaces, turn.

Row 19: Ch 10, dc in 8th stitch from hook, ch 2, dc in last dc of preceding row, 1 space, 1 block, 7 spaces, 1 block, 3 spaces, 1 block, 1 space, turn. 17 squares.

Row 20: 1 space, 1 block, 3 spaces, 2 blocks, 1 space, 1 block, 3 spaces, 3 blocks, 2 spaces, turn.

Row 21: Ch 10, dc in 8th stitch from hook, ch 2, dc in last dc of preceding row, 1 space, 5 blocks, 2 spaces, 3 blocks, 4 spaces, 1 block, 1 space, turn. 19 squares.
Row 22: 1 space, 1 block, 4 spaces, 2 blocks, 2 spaces, 3 blocks, 1 space, 2 blocks, 3 spaces, turn.
Row 23: Ch 10, dc in 8th stitch from hook, ch 2, dc in last dc of preceding row, 3 spaces, 1 block, 3 spaces, 2 blocks, 4 spaces, 1 block, 3 spaces, 1 block, 1 space, turn. 21 squares.
Row 24: Slip over 1 space, ch 3 for first dc, (1 block, 3 spaces) twice, 3 blocks, 3 spaces, 1 block, 5 spaces, turn. 20 squares.
Row 25: Ch 10, dc in 8th stitch from hook, ch 2, dc in last dc of preceding row, 5 spaces, 2 blocks, 2 spaces, 3 blocks, (3 spaces, 1 block) twice, turn. 22 squares.
Row 26: 4 spaces, 2 blocks, 1 space, 3 blocks, 3 spaces, 1 block, 8 spaces, turn.
Row 27: Slip over 2 spaces, 6 spaces, 3 blocks, 1 space, 5 blocks, 5 spaces, turn. 20 squares.
Row 28: 6 spaces, 3 blocks, 2 spaces, 1 block, 1 space, 1 block, 6 spaces, turn.
Row 29: Slip over 2 spaces, 10 spaces, 1 block, 5 spaces, 2 blocks, turn. 18 squares.
Row 30: 1 space, 2 blocks, 15 spaces, turn.
Row 31: Slip over 2 spaces, 12 spaces, 2 blocks, 2 spaces, turn. 16 squares.
Row 32: 1 space, 4 blocks, 11 spaces, turn.
Row 33: Slip over 2 spaces, 10 spaces, 4 blocks, turn. 14 squares.
Row 34: 3 blocks, 11 spaces, turn.
Row 35: Slip over 2 spaces, 11 spaces, 1 block, turn. 12 squares.
Row 36: 2 spaces, 2 blocks, 8 spaces, turn.
Row 37: Slip over 2 spaces, 7 spaces, 1 block, 2 spaces, turn. 10 squares.
Row 38: 4 blocks, 6 spaces, turn.
Row 39: Slip over 2 spaces, 7 spaces, 1 block, turn. 8 squares.

Row 40: 8 spaces, turn.
Row 41: Slip over 2 spaces, 6 spaces, turn. 6 squares.
Row 42: 6 spaces, turn.
Row 43: Slip over 2 spaces, 4 spaces, turn. 4 squares.
Row 44: 4 spaces, turn.
Row 45: Slip over 2 spaces, 2 spaces, turn. 2 squares.
Row 46: 2 spaces, turn and slip back over the 2 spaces; turn the corner and work along the side.
Row 47: Slip over 2 spaces, 5 spaces, 1 block, 3 spaces, 3 blocks, (3 spaces, 1 block) twice, chain 2, join to corner of last space of Row 23, turn. 21 squares.
Row 48: 1 space, 1 block, 3 spaces, 1 block, 4 spaces, 2 blocks, 3 spaces, 1 block, 5 spaces, turn.
Row 49: Slip over 2 spaces, 3 spaces, 2 blocks, 1 space, 3 blocks, 2 spaces, 2 blocks, 4 spaces, 1 block, 1 space, turn. 19 squares.
Row 50: 1 space, 1 block, 4 spaces, 3 blocks, 2 spaces, 5 blocks, 3 spaces, turn.
Row 51: Slip over 2 spaces, 2 spaces, 3 blocks, 3 spaces, 1 block, 1 space, 2 blocks, 3 spaces, 1 block, 1space, turn. 17 squares.
Row 52: 1 space, 1 block, 3 spaces, 1 block, 7 spaces, 1 block, 3 spaces, turn.
Row 53: Slip over 2 spaces, 13 spaces, 1 block, 1 space, turn. 15 squares.

Flying Goose
Row 54: 1 space, 1 block, 13 spaces, turn.
Row 55: Ch 10, dc in 8th stitch from hook, ch 2, dc in last dc of preceding row, 8 spaces, 1 block, 4 spaces, 1 block, 1 space, turn. 17 squares.
Row 56: 1 space, 1 block, 4 spaces, 1 block, 3 spaces, 2 blocks, 5 spaces, turn.

Row 57: Ch 10, dc in 8th stitch from hook, ch 2, dc in last dc of preceding row, 4 spaces, 4 blocks, 1 space, 3 blocks, 3 spaces, 1 block, 1 space, turn. 19 squares.

Row 58: 1 space, 1 block, 2 spaces, 2 blocks, (1 space, 3 blocks) twice, 5 spaces, turn.

Row 59: Ch 10, dc in 8th stitch from hook, ch 2, dc in last dc of preceding row, 1 space, 1 block, 2 spaces, 3 blocks, 1 space, 6 blocks, 3 spaces, 1 block, 1 space, turn. 21 squares.

Row 60: 1 space, 1 block, 7 spaces, 3 blocks, 1 space, 4 blocks, 4 spaces, turn.

Row 61: Ch 10, dc in 8th stitch from hook, ch 2, dc in last dc of preceding row, 3 spaces, 1 block, 2 spaces, (2 blocks, 1 space) twice, 3 blocks, 4 spaces, 1 block, 1 space, turn. 23 squares.

Row 62: 1 space, 1 block, 3 spaces, (2 blocks, 1 space) twice, 6 blocks, 6 spaces, turn.

Row 63: Slip over 2 spaces, 6 spaces, 11 blocks, 2 spaces, 1 block, 1 space, turn. 21 squares.

Row 64: 1 space, 1 block, (2 spaces, 1 block) twice, 1 space, 2 blocks, 2 spaces, 3 blocks, 5 spaces, turn.

Row 65: Slip over 2 spaces, 3 spaces, 2 blocks, 3 spaces, 1 block, 1 space, 4 blocks, 3 spaces, 1 block, 1 space, turn. 19 squares.

Row 66: 1 space, 1 block, 3 spaces, (1 block, 1 space) twice, 1 block, 4 spaces, 3 blocks, 2 spaces, turn.

Row 67: Slip over 2 spaces, 1 space, 1 block, 5 spaces, 4 blocks, 1 space, 1 block, 2 spaces, 1 block, 1 space, turn. 17 squares.

Row 68: 1 space, 1 block, 3 spaces, 2 blocks, 10 spaces, turn.

Row 69: Slip over 2 spaces, 10 spaces, 1 block, 2 spaces, 1 block, 1 space, turn. 15 squares.

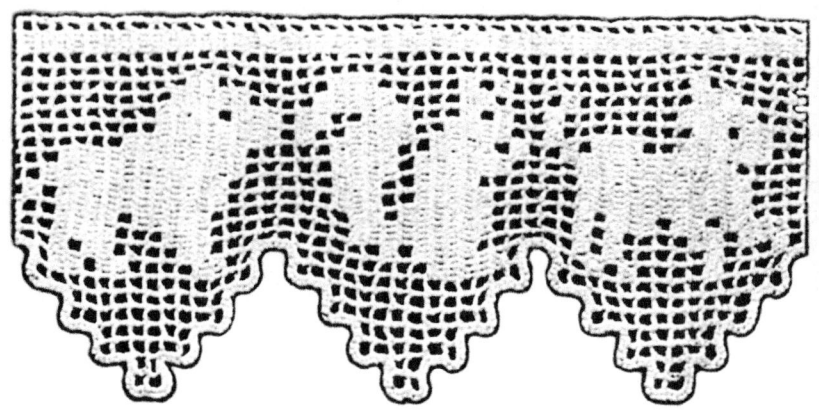

Horse

Row 70: 1 space, 1 block, 13 spaces, turn.

Row 71: Ch 10, dc in 8th stitch from hook, ch 2, dc in last dc of preceding row, 2 blocks, 11 spaces, 1 block, 1 space, turn. 17 squares.

Row 72: 1 space, 1 block, 5 spaces, 2 blocks, 4 spaces, 1 block, 3 spaces, turn.

Row 73: Ch 10, dc in 8th stitch from hook, ch 2, dc in last dc of preceding row, 3 spaces, 4 blocks, 1 space, 3 blocks, 4 spaces, 1 block, 1 space, turn. 19 squares.

Row 74: 1 space, 1 block, 3 spaces, 2 blocks, 1 space, 5 blocks, 6 spaces, turn.

Row 75: Ch 10, dc in 8th stitch from hook, ch 2, dc in last dc of preceding row, 3 spaces, 3 blocks, 1 space, 7 blocks, 3 spaces, 1 block, 1 space, turn. 21 squares.

Row 76: 1 space, 1 block, 2 spaces, 10 blocks, 7 spaces, turn.

Row 77: Ch 10, dc in 8th stitch from hook, ch 2, dc in last dc of preceding row, 8 spaces, 5 blocks, 1 space, 1 block, 4 spaces, 1 block, 1 space, turn. 23 squares.

Row 78: 1 space, 1 block, 7 spaces, 3 blocks, 11 spaces, turn.

Row 79: Slip over 2 spaces, 8 spaces, 4 blocks, 7 spaces, 1 block, 1 space, turn. 21 squares.

Row 80: 1 space, 1 block, 6 spaces, 5 blocks, 2 spaces, 1 block, 5 spaces, turn.

Row 81: Slip over 2 spaces, 4 spaces, 7 blocks, 6 spaces, 1 block, 1 space, turn. 19 squares.

Row 82: 1 space, 1 block, 6 spaces, 4 blocks, 3 spaces, 1 block, 3 spaces, turn.

Row 83: Slip over 2 spaces, 2 spaces, 6 blocks, 7 spaces, 1 block, 1 space, turn. 17 squares.

Row 84: 1 space, 1 block, 3 spaces, 1 block, 2 spaces, 1 block, 8 spaces, turn.

Row 85: Slip over 2 spaces, 7 spaces, 2 blocks, 4 spaces, 1 block, 1 space, turn. 15 squares.

Squirrel

Row 86: 1 space, 1 block, 13 spaces, turn.

Row 87: Ch 10, dc in 8th stitch from hook, ch 2, dc in last dc of preceding row, 6 spaces, 1 block, 6 spaces, 1 block, 1 space, turn. 17 squares.

Row 88: 1 space, 1 block, 2 spaces, 1 block, 1 space, 2 blocks, 1 space, 1 block, 5 spaces, 1 block, 1 space, turn.

Row 89: Ch 10, dc in 8th stitch from hook, ch 2, dc in last dc of preceding row, 1 space, 1 block, (1 space, 3 blocks) twice, 1 space, 1 block, 3 spaces, 1 block, 1 space, turn. 19 squares.

Row 90: 1 space, 1 block, 2 spaces, 12 blocks, 3 spaces, turn.

Row 91: Ch 10, dc in 8th stitch from hook, ch 2, dc in last dc of preceding row, 3 spaces, 9 blocks, 5 spaces, 1 block, 1 space, turn. 21 squares.

Row 92: 1 space, 1 block, 6 spaces, 8 blocks, 5 spaces, turn.

Row 93: Ch 10, dc in 8th stitch from hook, ch 2, dc in last dc of preceding row, 6 spaces, 6 blocks, 7 spaces, 1 block, 1 space, turn. 23 squares.

Row 94: 1 space, 1 block, 3 spaces, 2 blocks, 4 spaces, 2 blocks, 10 spaces, turn.

Row 95: Slip over 2 spaces, 6 spaces, 2 blocks, 3 spaces, 5 blocks, 3 spaces, 1 block, 1 space, turn. 21 squares.

Row 96: 1 space, 1 block, 2 spaces, 10 blocks, 7 spaces, turn.

Row 97: Slip over 2 spaces, 5 spaces, 7 blocks, 1 space, 2 blocks, 2 spaces, 1 block, 1 space, turn. 19 squares.

Row 98: 1 space, 1 block, 2 spaces, 2 blocks, 2 spaces, 4 blocks, 7 spaces, turn.

Row 99: Slip over 2 spaces, 10 spaces, 2 blocks, 3 spaces, 1 block, 1 space, turn. 17 squares.

Row 100: 1 space, 1 block, 4 spaces, 2 blocks, 9 spaces, turn.

Row 101: Slip over 2 spaces, 13 spaces, 1 block, 1 space, turn. 15 squares.

Lion

Row 102: 1 space, 1 block, 4 spaces, 2 blocks, 7 spaces, turn.

Row 103: Ch 10, dc in 8th stitch from hook, ch 2, dc in last dc of preceding row, 7 spaces, 2 blocks, 4 spaces, 1 block, 1 space, turn. 17 squares.

Row 104: 1 space, 1 block, 3 spaces, 5 blocks, 7 spaces, turn.

Row 105: Ch 10, dc in 8th stitch from hook, ch 2, dc in last dc of preceding row, 1 space, 1 block, 3 spaces, 5 blocks, 1 space, 1 block, 3 spaces, 1 block, 1 space, turn. 19 squares.

Row 106: 1 space, 1 block, 2 spaces, 12 blocks, 3 spaces, turn.

Row 107: Ch 10, dc in 8th stitch from hook, ch 2, dc in last dc of preceding row, 4 spaces, 11 blocks, 2 spaces, 1 block, 1 space, turn. 21 squares.

Row 108: 1 space, 1 block, 3 spaces, 9 blocks, 7 spaces, turn.

Row 109: Ch 10, dc in 8th stitch from hook, ch 2, dc in last dc of preceding row, 8 spaces, 7 blocks, 4 spaces, 1 block, 1 space, turn. 23 squares.

Row 110: 1 space, 1 block, 6 spaces, 5 blocks, 10 spaces, turn.

Row 111: Slip over 2 spaces, 5 spaces, 1 block, 3 spaces, 4 blocks, 6 spaces, 1 block, 1 space, turn. 21 squares.

Row 112: 1 space, 1 block, 7 spaces, 7 blocks, 5 spaces, turn.

Row 113: Slip over 2 spaces, 4 spaces, 6 blocks, 7 spaces, 1 block, 1 space, turn. 19 squares.

Row 114: 1 space, 1 block, 7 spaces, 5 blocks, 1 space, 1 block, 3 spaces, turn.

Row 115: Slip over 2 spaces, 1 space, 7 blocks, 7 spaces, 1 block, 1 space, turn. 17 squares.

Row 116: 1 space, 1 block, 8 spaces, 1 block, 6 spaces, turn.

Row 117: Slip over 2 spaces, 3 spaces, 1 block, 9 spaces, 1 block, 1 space, turn. 15 squares.

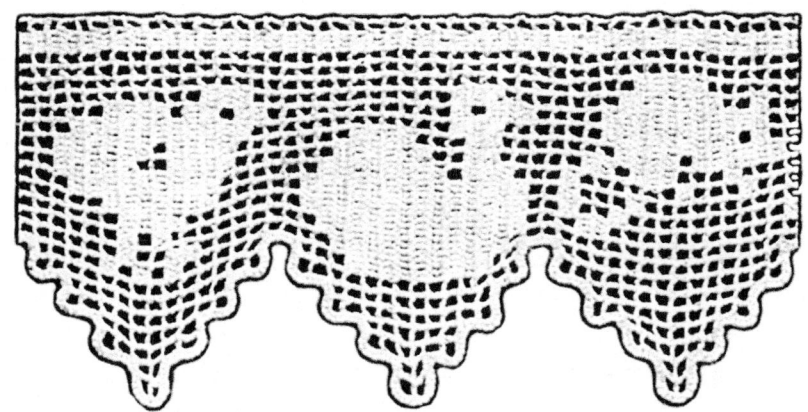

Mouse

Row 118: 1 space, 1 block, 10 spaces, 1 block, 2 spaces, turn.

Row 119: Ch 10, dc in 8th stitch from hook, ch 2, dc in last dc of preceding row, (6 spaces, 1 block) twice, 1 space, turn. 17 squares.

Row 120: 1 space, 1 block, 3 spaces, 4 blocks, 8 spaces, turn.

Row 121: Ch 10, dc in 8th stitch from hook, ch 2, dc in last dc of preceding row, 6 spaces, 1 block, (1 space, 1 block) twice, 4 spaces, 1 block, 1 space, turn. 19 squares.

Row 122: 1 space, 1 block, 4 spaces, 4 blocks, 9 spaces, turn.

Row 123: Ch 10, dc in 8th stitch from hook, ch 2, dc in last dc of preceding row, 10 spaces, 4 blocks, 3 spaces, 1 block, 1 space, turn. 21 squares.

Row 124: 1 space, 1 block, 2 spaces, 5 blocks, 12 spaces, turn.

Row 125: Ch 10, dc in 8th stitch from hook, ch 2, dc in last dc of preceding row, 10 spaces, 1 block, 2 spaces, 4 blocks, 2 spaces, 1 block, 1 space, turn. 23 squares.

Row 126: 1 space, 1 block, 2 spaces, 6 blocks, 13 spaces, turn.

Row 127: Slip over 2 spaces, 11 spaces, 6 blocks, 2 spaces, 1 block, 1 space, turn. 21 squares.

Row 128: 1 space, 1 block, 2 spaces, 6 blocks, 1 space, 1 block, 9 spaces, turn.

Row 129: Slip over 2 spaces, 6 spaces, 1 block, 3 spaces, 4 blocks, 3 spaces, 1 block, 1 space, turn. 19 squares.

Row 130: 1 space, 1 block, 4 spaces, 2 blocks, 1 space, 1 block, 3 spaces, 1 block, 5 spaces, turn.

Row 131: Slip over 2 spaces, 3 spaces, 1 block, 3 spaces, 1 block, 7 spaces, 1 block, 1 space, turn. 17 squares.

Row 132: 1 space, 1 block, 8 spaces, 3 blocks, 4 spaces, turn.

Row 133: Slip over 2 spaces, 13 spaces, 1 block, 1 space, turn. 15 squares.

Duck

Row 134: 1 space, 1 block, 13 spaces, turn.

Row 135: Ch 10, dc in 8th stitch from hook, ch 2, dc in last dc of preceding row, 1 space, 3 blocks, 4 spaces, 1 block, 4 spaces, 1 block, 1 space, turn. 17 squares.

Row 136: 1 space, 1 block, 4 spaces, 1 block, 3 spaces, 5 blocks, 2 spaces, turn.

Row 137: Ch 10, dc in 8th stitch from hook, ch 2, dc in last dc of preceding row, 1 space, 11 blocks, 3 spaces, 1 block, 1 space, turn. 19 squares.

Row 138: 1 space, 1 block, 3 spaces, 1 block, 1 space, 9 blocks, 3 spaces, turn.

Row 139: Ch 10, dc in 8th stitch from hook, ch 2, dc in last dc of preceding row, 3 spaces, 5 blocks, 3 spaces, 3 blocks, 3 spaces, 1 block, 1 space, turn. 21 squares.

Row 140: 1 space, 1 block, 8 spaces, 6 blocks, 5 spaces, turn.

Row 141: Ch 10, dc in 8th stitch from hook, ch 2, dc in last dc of preceding row, 5 spaces, 7 blocks, 7 spaces, 1 block, 1 space, turn. 23 squares.

Row 142: 1 space, 1 block, 6 spaces, 8 blocks, 7 spaces, turn.

Row 143: Slip over 2 spaces, 5 spaces, 8 blocks, 6 spaces, 1 block, 1 space, turn. 21 squares.

Row 144: 1 space, 1 block, 6 spaces, 8 blocks, 5 spaces, turn.

Row 145: Slip over 2 spaces, 3 spaces, 8 blocks, 6 spaces, 1 block, 1 space, turn. 19 squares.

Row 146: 1 space, 1 block, 7 spaces, 6 blocks, 4 spaces, turn.

Row 147: Slip over 2 spaces, 3 spaces, 4 blocks, 8 spaces, 1 block, 1 space, turn. 17 squares.

Row 148: 1 space, 1 block, 9 spaces, 2 blocks, 4 spaces, turn.

Row 149: Slip over 2 spaces, 13 spaces, 1 block, 1 space, turn. 15 squares.

Chicken

Row 150: 1 space, 1 block, 13 spaces, turn.

Row 151: Ch 10, dc in 8th stitch from hook, ch 2, dc in last dc of preceding row, 8 spaces, 1 block, 4 spaces, 1 block, 1 space, turn. 17 squares.

Row 152: 1 space, 1 block, 3 spaces, 3 blocks, 9 spaces, turn.

Row 153: Ch 10, dc in 8th stitch from hook, ch 2, dc in last dc of preceding row, 7 spaces, 3 blocks, 1 space, 1 block, 3 spaces, 1 block, 1 space, turn. 19 squares.

Row 154: 1 space, 1 block, 3 spaces, 7 blocks, 7 spaces, turn.

Row 155: Ch 10, dc in 8th stitch from hook, ch 2, dc in last dc of preceding row, 4 spaces, 1 block, 2 spaces, 6 blocks, 4 spaces, 1 block, 1 space, turn. 21 squares.

Row 156: 1 space, 1 block, 5 spaces, 6 blocks, 1 space, 2 blocks, 5 spaces, turn.

Row 157: Ch 10, dc in 8th stitch from hook, ch 2, dc in last dc of preceding row, 7 spaces, 4 blocks, 2 spaces, 2 blocks, 4 spaces, 1 block, 1 space, turn. 23 squares.

Row 158: 1 space, 1 block, 4 spaces, 3 blocks, 1 space, 3 blocks, 2 spaces, 1 block, 7 spaces, turn.

Row 159: Slip over 2 spaces, 6 spaces, 9 blocks, 4 spaces, 1 block, 1 space, turn. 21 squares.

Row 160: 1 space, 1 block, 4 spaces, 6 blocks, 3 spaces, 1 block, 5 spaces, turn.

Row 161: Slip over 2 spaces, 8 spaces, 4 blocks, 5 spaces, 1 block, 1 space, turn. 19 squares.

Row 162: 1 space, 1 block, 5 spaces, 4 blocks, 8 spaces, turn.

Row 163: Slip over 2 spaces, 7 spaces, 2 blocks, 6 spaces, 1 block, 1 space, turn. 17 squares.

Row 164: 1 space, 1 block, 15 spaces, turn.

Row 165: Slip over 2 spaces, 13 spaces, 1 block, 1 space, turn. 15 squares.

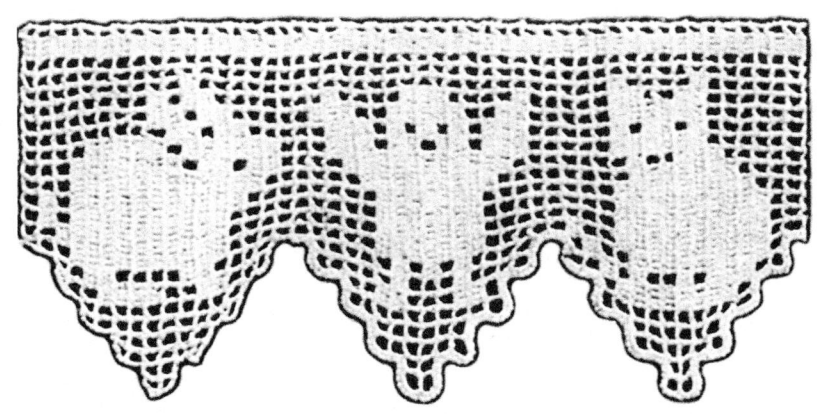

Cat

Row 166: 1 space, 1 block, 13 spaces, turn.

Row 167: Ch 10, dc in 8th stitch from hook, ch 2, dc in last dc of preceding row, 13 spaces, 1 block, 1 space, turn. 17 squares.

Row 168: 1 space, 1 block, 10 spaces, 4 blocks, 1 space, turn.

Row 169: Ch 10, dc in 8th stitch from hook, ch 2, dc in last dc of preceding row, 6 blocks, 9 spaces, 1 block, 1 space, turn. 19 squares.

Row 170: 1 space, 1 block, 8 spaces, 8 blocks, 1 space, turn.

Row 171: Ch 10, dc in 8th stitch from hook, ch 2, dc in last dc of preceding row, 1 space, 9 blocks, 7 spaces, 1 block, 1 space, turn. 21 squares.

Row 172: 1 space, 1 block, 2 spaces, 12 blocks, 1 space, 1 block, 3 spaces, turn.

Row 173: Ch 10, dc in 8th stitch from hook, ch 2, dc in last dc of preceding row, 3 spaces, 10 blocks, 1 space, 2 blocks, 3 spaces, 1 block, 1 space, turn. 23 squares.

Row 174: 1 space, 1 block, 4 spaces, 3 blocks, 1 space, 6 blocks, 1 space, 1 block, 5 spaces, turn.

Row 175: Slip over 2 spaces, 3 spaces, 1 block, 1 space, 6 blocks, 1 space, 3 blocks, 4 spaces, 1 block, 1 space, turn. 21 squares.

Row 176: 1 space, 1 block, 3 spaces, 2 blocks, 1 space, 10 blocks, 3 spaces, turn.

Row 177: Slip over 2 spaces, 1 space, 1 block, 2 spaces, 4 blocks, 2 spaces, 5 blocks, 2 spaces, 1 block, 1 space, turn. 19 squares.

Row 178: 1 space, 1 block, 14 spaces, 1 block, 2 spaces, turn.

Row 179: Slip over 2 spaces, 1 space, 1 block, 13 spaces, 1 block, 1 space, turn. 17 squares.

Row 180: 1 space, 1 block, 12 spaces, 1 block, 2 spaces, turn.

Row 181: Slip over 2 spaces, 13 spaces, 1 block, 1 space, turn. 15 squares.

Owl

Row 182: 1 space, 1 block, 13 spaces, turn.

Row 183: Ch 10, dc in 8th stitch from hook, ch 2, dc in last dc of preceding row, 6 spaces, 4 blocks, 3 spaces, 1 block, 1 space, turn. 17 squares.

Row 184: 1 space, 1 block, 4 spaces, 4 blocks, 7 spaces, turn.

Row 185: Ch 10, dc in 8th stitch from hook, ch 2, dc in last dc of preceding row, 6 spaces, 4 blocks, 5 spaces, 1 block, 1 space, turn. 19 squares.

Row 186: 1 space, 1 block, 7 spaces, 6 blocks, 2 spaces, 1 block, 1 space, turn.

Row 187: Ch 10, dc in 8th stitch from hook, ch 2, dc in last dc of preceding row, 1 space, 12 blocks, 4 spaces, 1 block, 1 space, turn. 21 squares.

Row 188: 1 space, 1 block, 3 spaces, 2 blocks, 1 space, 7 blocks, 6 spaces, turn.

Row 189: Ch 10, dc in 8th stitch from hook, ch 2, dc in last dc of preceding row, 5 spaces, 7 blocks, 1 space, 3 blocks, 3 spaces, 1 block, 1 space, turn. 23 squares.

Row 190: 1 space, 1 block, 3 spaces, 2 blocks, 1 space, 7 blocks, 8 spaces, turn.

Row 191: Slip over 2 spaces, 3 spaces, 12 blocks, 4 spaces, 1 block, 1 space, turn. 21 squares.

Row 192: 1 space, 1 block, 7 spaces, 6 blocks, 2 spaces, 1 block, 3 spaces, turn.

Row 193: Slip over 2 spaces, 8 spaces, 4 blocks, 5 spaces, 1 block, 1 space, turn. 19 squares.

Row 194: 1 space, 1 block, 4 spaces, 4 blocks, 9 spaces, turn.

Row 195: Slip over 2 spaces, 8 spaces, 4 blocks, 3 spaces, 1 block, 1 space, turn. 17 squares.

Row 196: 1 space, 1 block, 4 spaces, 1 block, 10 spaces, turn.

Row 197: Slip over 2 spaces, 13 spaces, 1 block, 1 space, turn. 15 squares.

Rabbit

Row 198: 1 space, 1 block, 13 spaces, turn.

Row 199: Ch 10, dc in 8th stitch from hook, ch 2, dc in last dc of preceding row, 5 spaces, 2 blocks, 6 spaces, 1 block, 1 space, turn. 17 squares.

Row 200: 1 space, 1 block, 6 spaces, 3 blocks, 6 spaces, turn.

Row 201: Ch 10, dc in 8th stitch from hook, ch 2, dc in last dc of preceding row, 5 spaces, 2 blocks, 1 space, 2 blocks, 5 spaces, 1 block, 1 space, turn. 19 squares.

Row 202: 1 space, 1 block, 4 spaces, 9 blocks, 1 space, 1 block, 2 spaces, turn.

Row 203: Ch 10, dc in 8th stitch from hook, ch 2, dc in last dc of preceding row, 2 spaces, 9 blocks, 1 space, 2 blocks, 3 spaces, 1 block, 1 space, turn. 21 squares.

Row 204: 1 space, 1 block, 2 spaces, (2 blocks, 1 space) twice, 6 blocks, 5 spaces, turn.

Row 205: Ch 10, dc in 8th stitch from hook, ch 2, dc in last dc of preceding row, 6 spaces, 6 blocks, 1 space, 2 blocks, 4 spaces, 1 block, 1 space, turn. 23 squares.

Row 206: 1 space, 1 block, 3 spaces, 2 blocks, 1 space, 7 blocks, 1 space, 1 block, 6 spaces, turn.

Row 207: Slip over 2 spaces, 4 spaces, 1 block, 1 space, 7 blocks, 6 spaces, 1 block, 1 space, turn. 21 squares.

Row 208: 1 space, 1 block, 6 spaces, 7 blocks, 1 space, 1 block, 4 spaces, turn.

Row 209: Slip over 2 spaces, 2 spaces, 9 blocks, 6 spaces, 1 block, 1 space, turn. 19 squares.

Row 210: 1 space, 1 block, 6 spaces, 8 blocks, 3 spaces, turn.

Row 211: Slip over 2 spaces, 2 spaces, 6 blocks, 7 spaces, 1 block, 1 space, turn. 17 squares.

Row 212: 1 space, 1 block, 11 spaces, 1 block, 3 spaces, turn.

Row 213: Slip over 2 spaces, 2 spaces, 2 blocks, 9 spaces, 1 block, 1 space, turn. 15 squares.

This brings you to the second corner. Repeat from the first section if the border is long enough for your square or spread, as you have made it. If not, repeat a straight section, or any preferred scallop or scallops, until it is of sufficient length, then repeat the corner, and continue.

Edging

Finish the edge with 3 sc in each space, 6 sc in corner spaces.

Chart

Chain 50.

Odd rows are worked left to right. Even rows are worked right to left.

Begin rows with ch 5 for the first space.

Refer to written instructions for increases and decreases, turning the corner, edging, and customizations.

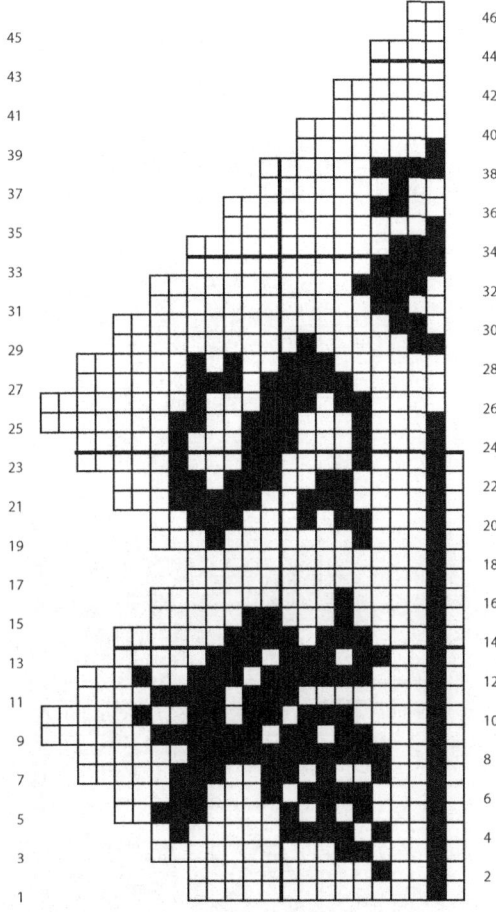

Animal Blocks Bedspread

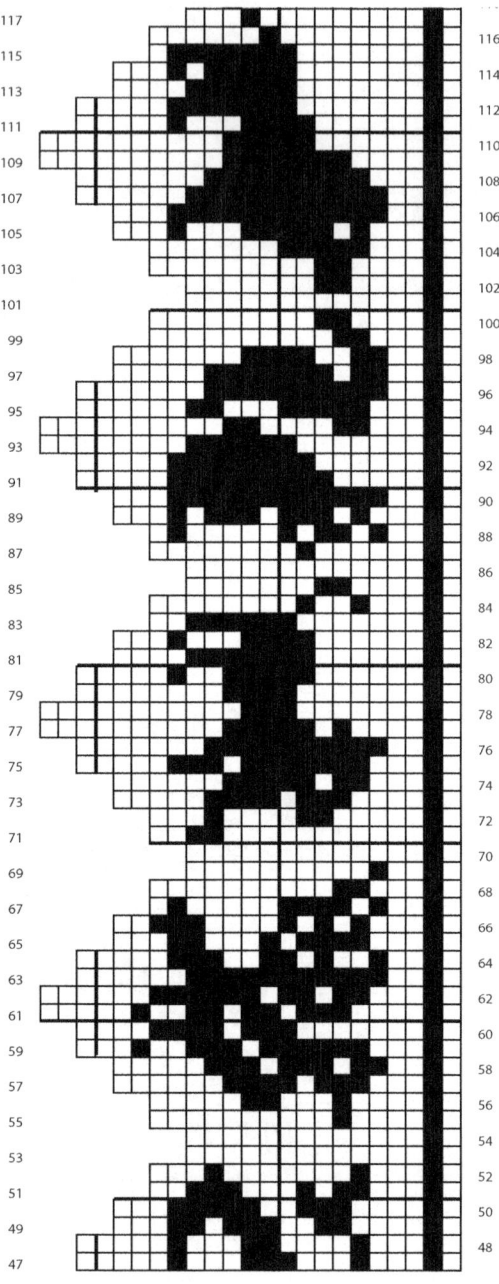

Zoo Border

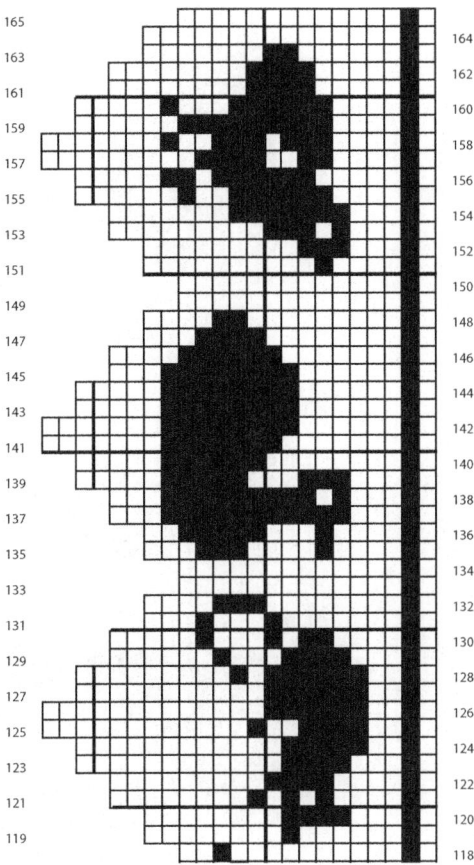

Animal Blocks Bedspread

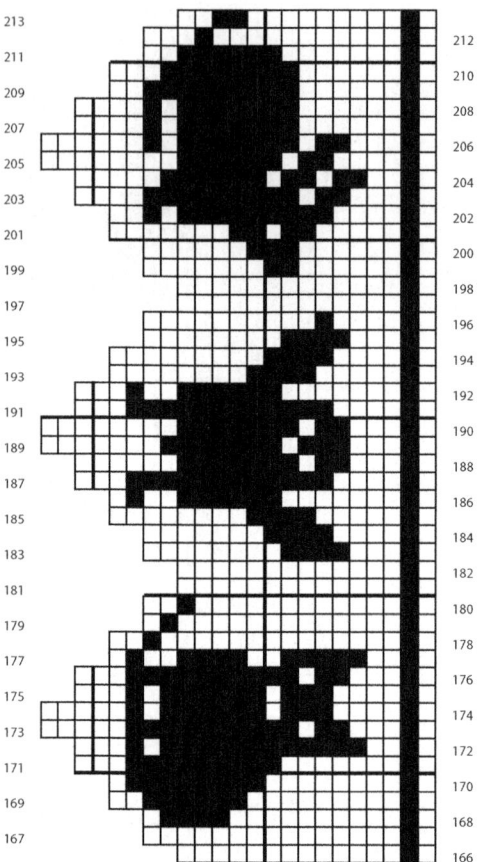

Optional Insertion

Shell: 3 dc, ch 2, 3 dc

Chain 21.
    Row 1: Shell in 6th stitch of chain, chain 11, skip 11, shell in next stitch, skip 2, dc in last stitch, turn.
    Row 2: Chain 4, shell in shell, chain 10, shell in shell, dc under chain at end of row, turn.
    Row 3: Chain 4, shell in shell, chain 5, sc in center of 11 chain of Row 1, chain 5, shell in shell, dc under chain at end, turn.
    Row 4: repeat Row 2.
    Row 5: Chain 4, shell in shell, chain 11, shell in shell, dc under chain at end, turn.
    Repeat from Row 2.

Join the squares in strips by means of the insertion, then run a row of insertion the entire length of strips.

Run ribbon under the clusters of chains and over the single chains.

Hints & Tips

Use the best thread. Don't try to save a few pennies on the thread. You're not just making lace, you're making an heirloom!

Wash your hands before you pick up your project to work on. Keeping your hands clean while you work will help to avoid stains on your piece of lace.

When you're finished, weave in ends of thread by pulling the thread through several stitches with your hook.

To block your lace, dampen it and use a warm iron to block it in to shape. I like to use a little bit of spray starch to finish it off.

Filet crochet patterns are made up of two elements. The first is the space, which is made up of a double crochet, chain two, skip two stitches, and double crochet in the next stitch. The second is the block, which is made of a double crochet, double crochet in the next two stitches, and double crochet in the next stitch.

When you make a block over a space from the previous row, just double crochet into the space. Don't worry about crocheting into each chain.

You can follow a chart instead of a written pattern (a chart is included with this pattern). When you use the chart, you just need to remember that the beginning of each row starts with either chain three (for a block) or chain five (for a space). You can also use the chart to check your progress if you're using the written instructions.

Visit http://claudiabotterweg.com/crochet for tips, hints and more about lace crochet.

I hope you enjoyed making this beautiful piece of lace. Tell your friends where you got the pattern.

About the Editor

Claudia Botterweg learned how to crochet in third grade, and by the time she left home for college she had completed 8 rows on a ripple afghan. At Ohio State, she found herself living across the street from a vintage clothing store, and spent most of her budget on vintage clothes. She began repairing clothes in exchange for store credit. One of her tasks was to make camisoles with vintage crocheted lace yokes.

After college, Claudia inherited a tin full of several used balls of tatting thread, a tatting shuttle, and a size 14 steel crochet hook from her grandmother. She made some lace edgings from an old crochet pattern book, became fascinated with lace, and graduated to making doilies. In the 1980s, she made hundreds of lace collars and sold them at craft fairs. She also designed her own camisole yokes and made camisoles to sell.

Recently, Claudia acquired a stack of vintage patterns. She has been busily translating the patterns from vintage instructions, making them easy for beginning and intermediate crocheters to read. She is writing instructions when only charts were provided, and making charts when only written instructions were provided.

Claudia hopes that a new generation of crocheters will learn how to make beautiful lace to decorate themselves, their friends and families, and their homes.

http://ClaudiaBotterweg.com

More Patterns from Claudia Botterweg
Grape & Leaf Altar Lace
Ivy Lace Scarf End
Beverly Lace & Insertion
Dogwood Blossom Lace Curtain
Two Peacocks Lace Curtain
Quilt Block Lace Edging & Insertion
Two Dragons Lace Curtain
Lyre Lace Scarf End
Butterfly Lace Camisole Yoke
Daffodil Lace Curtain
Rose Lace & Insertion
Daffodil Altar Lace
Garden Trellis Lace Centerpiece
Elegant Dragons Lace Curtain
Regal Peacocks Lace Curtain
Morning Glory Lace & Insertion
Nottingham Apple Lace Luncheon Set Filet Crochet Pattern
Lion Lace Panel Filet Crochet Pattern
Butterfly Lace Table Runner Filet Crochet Pattern
Crochet Journal
Knitting Journal
Quilting Journal
Rose Insertion Filet Crochet Pattern
Diamonds Insertion & Edging Filet Crochet Pattern
Tall Ship Lace Filet Crochet Pattern
Two Spring Lace Panels Filet Crochet Pattern
Tropical Flowers Lace Curtain Filet Crochet Pattern
Daisy Lace Corners Filet Crochet Pattern

Spirit of St. Louis Lace Panel Filet Crochet Pattern
Snowflake Square Lace Pillow Cover Filet Crochet Pattern
Clematis Lace Centerpiece Filet Crochet Pattern
26 Mix & Match Alphabet Insertions Filet Crochet Pattern
Sailor Boy Lace Panel Filet Crochet Pattern
INRI Altar Lace Filet Crochet Pattern
Seven Animal Insertions Filet Crochet Pattern
Rose and Butterfly Lace Border Filet Crochet Pattern

Printed in Great Britain
by Amazon